Forward to Beijing!

A Guide to the Summer Olympics

with a short history of the Games and lists of Gold Medal Winners in all Olympic Sports from the year 1988

by Verner Bickley

In August 2008, the twenty-ninth Summer Olympic Games was held in Beijing, The People's Republic of China. This is only the third time ever that this test and celebration of human endeavour has taken place in Asia.

Forward to Beijing! A Guide to the Summer Olympics was written in advance of this exciting event, and gives a brief history of the Games from their ancient origins in Greece to their revival in 1896. It surveys some of the triumphs enjoyed and difficulties encountered by the Olympic Movement over time and gives some of the highlights of Olympiads held from 1896 to 1984, including details of those athletes who won more than one gold medal each in any single one of these early modern Olympiads.

The Games first took place in Asia in 1964, in Tokyo, Japan, returning in 1988, twenty-four years later, this time to Seoul, Korea. Taking 1988 as a starting point, therefore, *Forward to Beijing!* gives a detailed account of several important aspects of the Olympic Games. Each of the twenty-eight Olympic sports from "Aquatics" to "Wrestling" is described with definitions of some of the special terms used and explanations of the rules that govern these sports, together with their associated disciplines. Here also, for every single Olympic sport, are the names of gold medal winners at these Games, and information about the country they represented.

Some Key Words for the discussion of each Olympic Sport are provided. Quizzes serve as a summary of the main points and as conversational openers.

Forward to Beijing! records many of the actions that the City of Beijing and the PRC undertook to ensure the success of the 2008 Games.

Somewhat light-heartedly, but also usefully, it features a number of situational conversations (with vocabulary and phrase book sections), all of which were considered to be helpful for visitors to the Games with no knowledge of Chinese and who would need to communicate in English during the Beijing 2008 Olympic Games. This was also considered useful to help those Chinese residents, who wished to communicate in English with foreign visitors — of whatever nationality — but who might have had little prior experience of doing so, to communicate more effectively. This was intended as our contribution to the Speak English Programme, introduced by the PRC to, "build up a favourable language environment" for the forthcoming Games. Now the Games are over, this feature continues to offer assistance to residents and visitors alike.

Forward to Beijing!
A Guide to the Summer Olympics

Verner Bickley

Proverse Hong Kong

Forward to Beijing! A Guide to the Summer Olympics with a short history of the Games and lists of Gold Medal Winners in all Olympic Sports from the year 1988
by Verner Courtenay Bickley
EBSCO edition, April 2012. ISBN: 978-988-8167-04-3
© Proverse Hong Kong April 2012
~~~
Previous Ebook editions:
24Reader E-book edition published by Proverse Hong Kong, December 2009. © Proverse Hong Kong December 2009.
ISBN: 978-988-18479-8-0
~~~
1st E-book edition (Mobibook) published by Proverse Hong Kong, 2008. © Proverse Hong Kong, 2008. ISBN 978-988-99668-7-4
Later redeployed as a Kindle book.
~~~
FIRST PRINT EDITION
First published in Hong Kong by Proverse Hong Kong, 29 February 2008.
ISBN 978-988-99668-3-6 © Proverse Hong Kong January 2008
Web site: www.proversepublishing.com
Distribution (Hong Kong and worldwide): The Chinese University Press of Hong Kong, The Chinese University of Hong Kong, Shatin, New Territories, Hong Kong, SAR.
E-mail: cup@cuhk.edu.hk Web site: www.chineseupress.com
Tel: [INT+852] 2609-6508; Fax: [INT+852] 2603-7355
Direct purchase link:
"http://www.chineseupress.com/asp/e_Book_card.asp?BookID=2318&Lang=E"

Distribution (**United Kingdom**): Enquiries and orders to Christine Penney, 28 West Street, Stratford-upon-Avon, Warwickshire CV37 6DN, UK. Email: chrisp@proversepublishing.com
Additional distribution: Proverse Hong Kong, P.O. Box 259, Tung Chung Post Office, Tung Chung, Lantau, NT, Hong Kong, SAR. E-mail: proverse@netvigator.com Web site: www.proversepublishing.com
Moral Rights: The right of Verner Bickley to be identified as the author of this book has been asserted by him in accordance with the Copyright, Designs and Patents Act 1988.
The right of Timothy Fok to be identified as the author of "Message for the Olympic Book", of A. de O. Sales to be identified as the author of the

"Preface" and of Chris Wardlaw to be identified as the author of "A Big Idea" has been asserted by each of them in accordance with the Copyright, Designs and Patents Act 1988. Editor: Gillian Bickley.
Printed in Hong Kong by Hong Kong Baptist University Printing Section.
Picture research, page design & copy-editing by Proverse Hong Kong.
Cover design by Alan Chow.
Portrait photo of Verner Bickley by Reginald Hunt.
Proverse Hong Kong acknowledges the professional assistance of:
Mr Danny K. C. Chow and Ms Coral Wong.
All rights reserved. No part of this publication may be reproduced, stored in a retrieval system, or transmitted in any form or by any means, electronic, mechanical, photocopying, recording or otherwise, without the prior written permission of the copyright owner.
The book is sold subject to the condition that it shall not, by way of trade or otherwise, be lent, re-sold, hired out or otherwise circulated without the author's or publisher's prior written consent in any form of binding or cover other than that in which it is published and without a similar condition including this condition being imposed on the subsequent owner or purchaser. Please request, in writing, any and all permissions from Proverse Hong Kong.

Proverse Hong Kong

British Library Cataloguing in Publication Data

Bickley, Verner Courtenay
 Forward to Beijing! : a guide to the Summer Olympics : with
 a short history of the Games and lists of gold medal
 winners in all Olympic sports from the year 1988
 1. Olympic Games (29th : 2008 : Beijing, China) 2. Olympics
 - Miscellanea 3. Olympics - Medals 4. English language -
 Conversation and phrase books
 I. Title
 796.4'8

 ISBN-13: 9789889966836

Message from Mr Timothy Fok

SPORTS FEDERATION & OLYMPIC COMMITTEE OF HONG KONG, CHINA

THE PRESIDENT

Message for the Olympic Book

Beijing will emerge as one of the most modern cities without forsaking its tradition through these Olympics and their preparations. For many, going anywhere outside their own familiar hearth can be a daunting experience. Beijing is perhaps even more prohibiting than some because the city is so vast, the culture is so rich and the language, mandarin, may be novel, especially for those coming for the first time and from far away.

This book in your hand is a handy primer, a guide, a digest that should act as a sort of cultural and linguistic compass to help visitors navigate the labyrinth of streets, alleys and boulevards with signs that may appear to the uninitiated as absolutely baffling. The discovery of Beijing requires a little time and a bit of a challenge but then this test of will and curiosity is the very essence of travel for it rewards the intrepid with many surprising encounters and serendipitous treasures to go with the photographs and sweeten the memories.

The Olympiad of 2008 will engender for the citizens of Beijing a chance to learn through more contact with the visitors with whom they are so eager to meet. Among the ideals embodied in the Olympic movement is that of the desire to create international goodwill, cooperation and peace. Everyone who comes to Beijing will be transformed thus into an ambassador for his or her country. A learning of even a few phrases will so please the Chinese people who want these Games to be cherished as those that bring the world to them and them to it. Welcome to Beijing and may you return again and again as well as spread the word, in mandarin or whatever language, that the people here are cordial and the sights and sounds are unforgettable.

Timothy Fok

Athens 2004 Olympiad: Flag Presentation Ceremony, Hong Kong. The Hon. Mr Timothy FOK Tsun Ting, SBS, GBS, JP and The Hon. Dr Arnaldo de Oliveira SALES, GBM, JP. *Photo Courtesy SFOCHKC.* ~

The Hon. Dr de Sales celebrated his 88th birthday in January 2008. Born in Guangzhou, Southern China, Dr Sales, a Portuguese national, studied in Hong Kong and has lived in Hong Kong since 1945. (He spent his early twenties, during the Second World War, in Macau.) Of his life's work, he said, "My life-long effort has revolved around children. My hope is to raise the quality of living of our local people in their neighbourhood, and to bring them happier lives."

The Sports Federation & Olympic Committee of Hong Kong, China (SF&OC) was founded in late 1949 under the name, "Amateur Sports Federation of Hong Kong", with HSBC banker, Sir Arthur Morse, as inaugural president. In 1951, on the initiative of Sandy Duncan, Honorary Secretary of the British Olympic Association, it was recognized as a separate member of the International Olympic Committee (IOC).[1] Sir Arthur Morse retired from HSBC in 1952 and Mr de Sales, then secretary general of the SF&OC, became its second president, continuing in that position, with great energy, dedication, courage and skill, for forty-six years or so, earning the indisputable title, "Father of Hong Kong Sport".

Mr de Sales was active in negotiating a smooth transition from the colonial to the post-colonial period for Hong Kong sports, signing an agreement with then IOC President Juan Antonio Samaranch, which the two men confirmed a few days after the return of Hong Kong to China. As a result, Hong Kong continues to compete in international sports as a separate entity, now known as, "Hong Kong, China".

When China resumed the exercise of sovereignty over Hong Kong in 1997, the Federation was renamed, "Amateur Sports Federation and Olympic Committee of Hong Kong, China". In 1999, members voted to remove the word, "Amateur".

Apart from his staunch strong leadership for almost five decades, Dr de Sales will certainly be remembered for his heroic part in rescuing members of the Hong Kong delegation during the Black September terrorist occupation of athletes' quarters at the 1972 Munich Olympics. "Police warned me it would be too dangerous to approach the building, because I might be held as hostage, and get killed. However, as Chef de Mission, my duties were not limited to posing for photographs and shaking hands with other delegates. I had to fulfill my duties as a leader, especially when it was dangerous. I needed to try my best to protect every member of my team."

Hearty and generous support for Hong Kong Sports was consistently given through the years by the late Dr Henry Fok Ying-tung.

In March 1998, Dr Henry Fok's son, Timothy Fok Tsun Ting, became, unopposed, the third president of SF&OC and has already made his mark. Timothy proposed to the Committee and subsequently supported the interchange of sporting activities between Hong Kong and China. As a legislator, he has grown support within the Legislative Council for increased government funding for sports development, and to produce and promote long-term sports development projects to benefit the entire Hong Kong community. In 2001 he was elected a member of the International Olympic Committee.

It is largely through the efforts of the Hon. Timothy Fok and his cadre of SF&OC elected officers, that Hong Kong will host the equestrian events in the summer of 2008, as part of the Beijing Summer Olympic Games; and in 2009 will host the East Asian Games.

Preface by the Hon. Dr. Arnaldo de Oliveira Sales

Preface

During the almost sixty years that I have been active in the Hong Kong sports community and in the Olympic Games as an administrator and official representing Hong Kong, I have believed firmly in the Olympic ideals. I have seen how the aspirations enshrined in these ideals inspire athletes, coaches and spectators alike. I have witnessed continuing and concrete evidence of the beneficial impact of participating in sports at any level – and particularly at the highest level of competition, which successive Olympic Games provide – particularly on the young people of the world.

Athletes learn how to focus on a goal and how to make extreme personal sacrifices as they aim for that goal. They learn how to prioritise among possible activities, relationships and ambitions. They develop the highest levels of athletic skill, certainly. But they also gain in confidence and self-respect as well and – equally valuable – they learn how to value and respect others.

Those who follow sport and particularly the Olympic Games as spectators find in these athletes objects for admiration, who inspire them to pursue worthy goals of their own in their own spheres of action and achievement.

Athletes, coaches, supporters, officials, spectators – whatever the part we play, from whichever of the myriad families of the world we come, to whichever culture or condition of men we belong – we learn and experience that sporting endeavour and the successive Olympiads which fuel that endeavour can and do unite us under the umbrella of universally acceptable ideals.

Hong Kong China has come a long way from the early years after the Second World War. In 2008, for the first time, Hong Kong athletes participate in the Olympic Games on the soil of their Motherland, whether in Beijing or in the Equestrian events to be held in Hong Kong.

Preface by the Hon. Dr. Arnaldo de Oliveira Sales

The disappointment felt in 1993 when China lost her bid to host the 2000 Olympic Games was extreme. The euphoria experienced in 2001 when the bid for the 2008 Games was won has for several years acted as a spur to excellence in many areas of personal, sporting and civic endeavour. Let the Games commence!

I congratulate Dr Verner Bickley, the author of this book, *Forward to Beijing! A Guide to the Summer Olympics*, for realizing, in the early 1990s, that the Summer Olympics would certainly come to China, and for understanding the considerable importance of this event. For well over a decade, he has sustained his conscientious interest. The result is this interesting, varied and helpful book, which suitably informs and prepares us ahead of the 2008 Summer Olympics. The value of Dr Bickley's work will certainly continue beyond this event, as a tool to understand future Olympiads as well.

The Hon. Dr Arnaldo de Oliveira Sales, GBM, JP
November 2007

Chairman of the Hong Kong Olympic Academy
and
Hon. Life President of the Sports Federation and Olympic Committee of Hong Kong, China

"A Big Idea" by Chris Wardlaw

A Big Idea

Sports can reflect human endeavour and human spirit as its best. For sport to be inspirational it must be founded on a set of values, which are universal. These values are inclusiveness, perseverance, tolerance, commitment and sportsmanship. The history of the Olympic Games has led them to become the pinnacle of sport. The Beijing Olympic Games will begin at 8pm, August 8, 2008, an auspicious moment. Like millions of others I will be watching.

I have been very fortunate to have had direct involvement in the Olympic movement over my lifetime. I remember vividly being a junior secondary student at a school in Melbourne, Victoria. Ron Clarke, Australia's great world-record-breaking distance runner spoke at our Speech Day. He said each of us had the potential to be "Olympian" – not just in sport, but to be truly excellent in other fields such as the arts, sciences, mathematics, languages.

A few years later I began my Olympic journey. I lined up on the starting line in the 10,000m at Montreal in 1976. I had trained very hard for years for that moment. I represented myself and my country, but especially my peers and training colleagues who had run many, many kilometres in practice with me. Preparing for that moment had taught me so much about myself; my emotions, my character; how resolute I could be in the moments of crisis in confidence that would surely come and whether I could do my best regardless of any obstacles in my way.

At Montreal I was a spectator as well as participant when I was given a ticket to witness Romania's Nadia Comanech, the gymnast whose "perfection" forced the sport to change its judging criteria. Comanech was asked how she achieved such heights of performance. In faltering English she said, "My head is full of getting it exactly right". Those who excel in sports, indeed in any field, knew what she was saying.

"A Big Idea" by Chris Wardlaw

I changed roles from athlete to personal coach, to team coach through the Games of Moscow, Seoul, Barcelona and Atlanta. The culmination of an Olympic life was my appointment as Head Coach of Australia's Track and Field Team at the 2000 Sydney Olympics. The joy and sense of achievement that Australians felt in hosting the Olympics was palpable.

More countries will participate at Beijing next year than are members of the United Nations. Women will make up fifty percent of participants as against none at all in the first modern games back in 1896. The Games both reflect and have contributed to universal values of inclusion which global cooperation and citizenship require.

By a twist of fate I will be in Hong Kong this year when it becomes part of the Olympic City by hosting the Equestrian Events. I will also be in the "Birds Nest" in Beijing when Liu Xiang, China's wonderful 110-metre hurdler defends his Olympic Crown. My role then is clearly as a sports fan. I can remind myself that, "excellence can come second", as the gap between gold and silver in that race is likely to be one hundredth of a second.

The Olympic Games is more than a major event. It is a big idea. Inspirational moments reverberate down through time. Beijing will remain an Olympic City forever, and many young people will be touched by the Olympic spirit of faster, higher, stronger (*citius, altius, fortius*) in and beyond sports.

Verner Bickley's book gives us, in an interesting way, basic tools for understanding the history, progress and conduct of this world-class event, which brings together so many aspects of human endeavour and achievement.

Chris Wardlaw
Olympic Games 1976 (10, 000m finalist) 1980 (marathon)
Head Coach, Australian Track and Field Team, 2000 Olympic Games[2]

Table of Contents

Forward to Beijing! A Guide to the Summer Olympics by Verner Bickley – Table of Contents

Message: The Hon. Timothy Fok, SBS, GBS, JP, President of the Sports Federation and Olympic Committee of Hong Kong, China		v
Preface: The Hon. Dr Arnaldo de Oliveira Sales, GBM, JP Honorary Life President of the Sports Federation and Olympic Committee of Hong Kong, China		vii
"A Big Idea": Chris Wardlaw, Head Coach, Australian Track and Field Team, 2000 Olympic Games		ix
	Table of Illustrations w. acknowledgements	xiii
	Acknowledgements	xvi
	Introduction	1
Chapter One	The Olympic Games: A Brief History.	3
Chapter Two	The Modern Olympic Movement.	11
Chapter Three	1896 to 1984: Some Highlights; including winners of more than one gold medal at any one early modern Olympiad. **1988 to 2008** Descriptions of all 28 Olympic sports held with their Rules. Definitions of special terms and key words. Lists of gold medal winners and the countries they represented. Quizzes.	29
Chapter Four	Aquatics to Athletics swimming, synchronized swimming, diving, synchronized diving, water polo, archery, athletics (field, track), decathlon, heptathlon.	37
Chapter Five	Badminton to Cycling badminton, baseball, basketball, beach volleyball, boxing, canoe / kayak (flat-water, slalom), cycling, road races, time trial races, mountain bike cross-country, track races, madison, keirin, BMX.	63
Chapter Six	Equestrian to Football equestrian (show-jumping, cross-country, dressage), fencing, football (soccer)	93

Table of Contents

Chapter Seven	Gymnastics to Judo artistic gymnastics, rhythmic gymnastics, trampoline, handball, hockey (field hockey), judo	107
Chapter Eight	Modern Pentathlon to Softball modern pentathlon: – pistol shooting, fencing (épée), swimming, horse-riding (show-jumping), running (cross-country); rowing, sailing, shooting, softball	129
Chapter Nine	Table Tennis to Wrestling table tennis, taekwondo, tennis, triathlon (swimming, cycling, running), volleyball, weightlifting, wrestling (Freestyle, Greco-Roman)	155
Chapter Ten	China and the Olympic Games	185
Chapter Eleven	The Olympics in the Hong Kong Media	195
	Language and other Notes for Olympic Visitors & Hosts	
Language One	Communicate! Survive in English in Beijing!	197
Language Two	Common words and expressions	205
Language Three	Visitors and Volunteers: some questions and answers	209
Language Four	The Hong Kong Visitors	212
Language Five	Important signs and notices in English	221
Language Six	Abbreviations for Olympic Terms	222
Language Seven	Special Olympic words and expressions	224
Language Eight	Abbreviations for International Sporting Bodies	225
Visitors' Notes 1	Useful Web Sites	226
Visitors' Notes 2	Time differences and measurements	227
Visitors' Notes 3	The Olympic Sports	228
	A Note on Olympic Studies Facilities	229
	Key to Quizzes	231
	References	236
	Notes	237
	Short Index	238
	About the Author and his work	239
	Proverse Books & About Proverse Hong Kong	241

Forward to Beijing! A Guide to the Summer Olympics   xiii

Table of Illustrations & Illustration Acknowledgements

Table of Illustrations

KEY

Athens = Olympic Games, 13-29 August 2004, held in Athens, Greece.
Doha = Asian Games, 1-15 December 2007, held in Doha, capital of Qatar, United Arab Emirates.
L = left. R = right. R1 = furthest to the right. R2 = next to the furthest to the right. Etc.

The Games of the XXVIII Olympiad (Athens 2004) – Flag Presentation Ceremony at Hong Kong. The Hon. Mr Timothy FOK Tsun Ting, SBS, GBS, JP and The Hon. Dr Arnaldo de Oliveira SALES, GBM, JP. *SFOCHKC*.	vi
The Temple of Heavenly Peace, Beijing. Beijing's bid to host the 2000 Olympiad included this temple in its logo. *PVHK*.	xv
Dr J. M. Park, arriving at Queen's Pier with the Olympic Flame, 1964. Typhoon Ruby was just beginning. *HKSAR Government*.	10
The Games of the XXVIII Olympiad (Athens 2004) – Flag Presentation Ceremony at Hong Kong. Group includes then Chief Executive The Hon. TUNG Chee Wah, The Hon. Timothy FOK Tsun Ting, SBS, GBS, JP, The Hon. Dr Arnaldo de Oliviera SALES, GBM, JP. *SFOCHKC*.	28
Mr Allan CHIANG, then Hong Kong Postmaster General, and Mr Timothy FOK, President, Sports Federation & Olympic Committee of Hong Kong, China. Preview Ceremony at the Hong Kong Central Post Office for the "2004 Olympic Games" Stamp Sheetlet. *SFOCHKC*.	28
Hannah WILSON. Aquatics, Athens. *SFOCHKC*.	36
LEUNG Chun Wai (R1); LAU Yu Leong (R2). Running, Doha. *SFOCHKC*.	36
LO Ting Wai (L) & SO Sau Wah (R). Canoeing, Doha. *SFOCHKC*.	62
WONG Kam Po (L1). Road Cycling, Doha. *SFOCHKC*.	62
Equestrian Event, Doha. *SFOCHKC*.	92
Women's Hockey, Doha. *SFOCHKC*.	106
CHAN Ka Man (L). Women's Judo, Doha. *SFOCHKC*.	106
Lee Lai Shan. Wind-surfing, Athens. *SFOCHKC*.	128
Forward to Beijing! A Guide to the Summer Olympics	xiv

Table of Illustrations & Illustration Acknowledgements

KO Lai Chak & LI Ching, men's table-tennis doubles silver medal winners. Awards ceremony, Athens. *SFOCHKC*.	184
Former Star Ferry underpass poster. *PVHK*.	220
Dr W. P. Brookes (L). Thomas Sabin (R). *WOS*.	238
(Top L) Aquatics, Doha. *SFOCHKC*.	243
CHIU Wing Yin (Centre L). Tennis, Doha. *SFOCHKC*.	243
YIP Ching Yee. (Top L) Judo, Doha. *SFOCHKC*.	243
LEE Lai-shan and the Hong Kong Team arriving back in Hong Kong from the 13th Asian Games, held in Bangkok, 1998. (Bottom) *HKSAR Government*.	243
SZE Hang Yu. (Top L) Aquatics, Athens. *SFOCHKC*.	244
KOON Wai Chee and LI Wing Mui. Women's badminton doubles, Athens. (Top R) *SFOCHKC*.	244
Welcome Home Ceremony for Hong Kong, China Delegation to Athens. LI Ching (L). KO Lai Chak (R). *SFOCHKC*.	244
HEI Zhi Hong, Taekwondo, Doha. (Bottom) *SFOCHKC*.	244
From L: Equestrian event, Doha (also p. 92). WONG Kam Po, Cycling, Athens. WANG Chen, Badminton, Athens. Lee Lai Shan, Wind-surfing, Athens (also p. 128). LAU Yu Leong, Running, Doha (also p. 36). *All photos SFOCHKC*.	cover (front)
National Stadium, Beijing, 23 August 2007. By Tee Meng.	cover

Illustration Acknowledgements

We acknowledge the HKSAR Government as the source of photographs indicated by "HKSAR Government", "The Sports Federation & Olympic Committee of Hong Kong, China" as the source of photographs indicated by "SFOCHKC" and the Wenlock Olympian Society as the source of the photographs indicated by "WOS". We are grateful for the kind permission given by each of these rights holders to reproduce their photographs in this book. "PVHK" indicates photographs belonging to Proverse Hong Kong.

Rights and Licences

The photograph of the Beijing National Stadium ("The Birds' Nest") by Tee Meng has been uploaded to Wikimedia by the photographer, and licensed by him under the GFDL. It has been released by Wikimedia under the GNU Free Documentation License and is reproduced here also under a GFDL licence.

Forward to Beijing! A Guide to the Summer Olympics   xv

Table of Illustrations & Illustration Acknowledgements

The icons for the various Beijing Olympic Games official events (pp. 61, 91,105, 127, 154, 183 below) are derived from the set of 35 icons, "Beauty of Seal Characters", co-designed by professors and students from the Chinese Central Academy of Fine Arts and the Fine Arts School of Qinghua University, which were officially released in China in August 2006. These pictograms, together with several sets of pictograms used at previous Olympic Games, are found on the official website of the BEIJING 2008 Olympic Games - Games of the XXIX Olympiad, 8-24 August 2008.
(http://en.beijing2008.com/63/32/column212033263.shtml)

We have taken all possible care to seek and acknowledge all necessary permissions. If, inadvertently, we have infringed any rights, we apologise and will take pains to correct this in any later edition.

The Temple of Heavenly Peace, Beijing. *PVHK.*
~ Beijing's bid to host the 2000 Olympiad included this temple in its logo.

Table of Illustrations & Illustration Acknowledgements

Acknowledgements

The Author and Publishers are most grateful to The Hon. Timothy Fok Tsun Ting, SBS, GBS, JP, President of the Sports Federation and Olympic Committee of Hong Kong, for his Message, to The Hon. Dr Arnaldo de Oliveira Sales, GBM, JP, Chairman of the Hong Kong Olympic Academy and Hon. Life President of the Sports Federation and Olympic Committee of Hong Kong, China, for his Preface and to Mr Chris Wardlaw, Head Coach, Australian Track and Field Team, 2000 Olympic Games, for his personal essay, A Big Idea.

We gratefully acknowledge support from Dr Hari N. Harilela, GBS, OBE, JP.

We acknowledge help and/or sponsorship given by individuals and organizations listed below:
China System Co. Ltd., Hong Kong. Mrs Joan Hayes, Whitchurch, Shropshire, United Kingdom. Hong Kong Baptist University: Professor Leung Mee Lee (Director, Centre for Olympic Studies); Professor Terry Yip (Department of English Language and Literature); Mr Danny Chow (Printing Section); Mr Henry So, Mr S. H. Tong (ITSC); Ms Koolly L. S. Ko (President and Vice Chancellor's Office). Hong Kong Public Records Office (Mr Bernard Hui, Ms Cammy Wong and colleagues). Information Services Department Photo Library, Government of the Hong Kong SAR (Mr William Ho & colleagues). Information Services Department, Government of the Hong Kong SAR (Ms Yung Yuen-han). Sports Federation & Olympic Committee of Hong Kong, China: Secretary General Mr Pang Chung, Senior Sports Executive Mr Leo P. K. Lam. University of Hong Kong: Dr Leo Francis Hoye (School of Education); Ms Denise Wong, Manager (Media) External Relations Office; Mrs Sylvia Cheung, External Relations Office; Mr Simon Lo, Assistant Director of the Institute of Human Performance. Office of Mr Timothy Fok: Ms Noel Lee. Office of the Hon. Mr A. de O. Sales: Ms Cindy Tse. P-Solution (HK) Ltd. Mrs Isobel Park. Ms Jessica Park. Mr Geoffrey Roper. Dr Vio & Partners. Wenlock Olympian Society, Shropshire, United Kingdom: Helen Clare Cromarty (PR & Sponsorship Secretary), Peter Thompson (Secretary).

Introduction

In 2008, from 8 to 24 August, the twenty-ninth Summer Olympic Games will be held in Beijing. Chapter One of this book gives a brief history of the Games from their origin in ancient Greece to their revival in 1896. In the latter year, the modern Olympics began modestly when 245 athletes from 13 countries took part in 42 events in Athens. In the same city, in 2004, more than 10,000 competitors participated in over 270 events.

Chapter Two contains a survey of some of the triumphs enjoyed and difficulties encountered by the Olympic Movement since its early days.

Chapter Three recalls some of the highlights of the Olympic Games, held at four-year intervals from 1896 until 1984, excepting 1916, 1940 and 1944, when war intervened.

In 1964, the Games had their Asian debut in Tokyo and Japan invested very heavily in their success. Among the innovative features provided were a Judo hall designed in the style of a Japanese temple and a unique swimming stadium described by the then IOC President, Avery Brundage as, "a cathedral of sports".

In 1988, the summer Olympic Games were returned to Asia (they were held in Seoul, Korea) after an absence of twenty-four years. In this "Foreword" to Beijing, 1988 is therefore taken as the starting point for a detailed account of important aspects of the Olympic Games.

In Chapters Four to Nine, you will find short descriptions of all the events held from 1988 up to and including the Athens Games of 2004. Each Olympic sport — from "Aquatics" to "Weightlifting" — is described with definitions of some of the special terms used ("Useful Terms") and Some Key Words. There are explanations of the rules that govern each of the 28 sports and their associated disciplines ("Rules of the Games"). Here also are lists of the individual athletes or teams in each Olympic sport,

Introduction

who have won gold medals, and the country they represented.

The "content" of the 2008 Beijing Games is substantially the same as that adopted for the 2004 Athens Games, except that there will be nine new events. Marathon swimming events for men and women will be added to the swimming discipline. Doubles events in tennis will be replaced by Team Events (women and men). Women will be included in the 3,000 metre steeplechase. Men's Team Foil and women's Team Épée will be replaced by women's team foil and women's Team Sabre.

Chapter Ten records many of the actions being taken in Beijing to ensure the success of the Games.

Chapter Eleven gives a flavour of how the Hong Kong media is focusing more and more on the Beijing Olympics.

In each of Chapters One to Ten there is a quiz intended to serve both as a summary of the main points and to provide conversational openers. A key is provided at the back of the book.

Eight Language sections follow. Language One features situational conversations as a helpful guide for communicating more effectively in English in the Olympic setting. Two contains a list of useful words and expressions. Three provides useful models of questions and answers. Four is a series of dialogues, in which Hong Kong visitors seek and receive information about Hong Kong and the Olympic Games in Hong Kong from different informants. Five to Eight provide examples of signs and notices, explanations of the abbreviations used for Olympic terms and refer to certain official sporting associations and a list of special Olympic words and expressions. All eight Language sections support the Chinese Speak English Programme, introduced to, "build up a favourable language environment", for the Beijing Games.

Verner Bickley
November 2007

Chapter One

THE OLYMPIC GAMES

A Brief History
There are many legends about the origins of the Olympic Games, but most historians agree that they were a celebration of Zeus, the King of the ancient Greek Gods. There are records to show that the first Games took place in 776 B.C. but there is also some evidence that Greek festivals celebrating athletes, music and religion were held centuries before that date.[3]

It does seem certain that, from 776 onwards, the Games were held every four years in Olympia, a sanctuary in the Peloponnese where there were many monuments and temples, including the temple of Zeus. Many people worshipped Zeus as the supreme god, the god of weather, the ruler and protector of the family and (in the modern sense) the "patron" of the Games.

At first, sprinting was the only sport offered in the ancient Games. The runners ran the length of the stadium, covering a distance of 192 metres. Later came chariot races, boxing, discus and javelin throwing, the long jump, wrestling, boxing and various equestrian events.

As time went on, sprinting was diversified. In one race, the competitors wore full battle armour and from 729 BC participants were obliged to compete in the nude (for safety reasons)!

In a famous ode, the Greek poet Pindar referred to a boxer named Diagoras as, "this straight-fighting, tremendous man" and Strabo, a Greek geographer, described the wrestler, Milo of Kroton, as "the most illustrious of athletes".

Otherwise, very little is known about the men who took part in the ancient Olympic Games.

In 393 AD, the Christian Emperor, Theodosios I, proscribed household gods, issued edicts directed against heretics;

Chapter One: The Olympic Games

condemned all worship of idols and abolished the Olympic Games on the grounds that they honoured Zeus, the pagan god.

Robert Dover's Olympics

The ancient Games in Greece had lasted for almost twelve centuries, in both good times and bad. After they were banned, boxing, wrestling, riding and other activities continued to be popular but the formal Greek Olympics themselves perished, although an attempt was made to revive them in a different form in 17th century England.

In 1612, in Chipping Campden, a small village in a hilly region of middle England, a lawyer named Robert Dover introduced a series of games that eventually included not only running, leaping and jumping, but also horse-racing, coursing, pitching the bar and hammer, hunting, dancing and card games! Twenty years or so after these annual Games began, a book of poems about Dover's "Olimpick" (*sic*) Games was published by a certain Matthew Walbancke. The book contained verses by respected writers such as Michael Drayton, as well as the playwrights, Thomas Heywood and Ben Jonson. In lighthearted manner, one of the other contributors, Nicholas Wallington, dedicated his contribution "To the Great Inventor and Champion of English Olimpicks, Pythics, Nemicks, Isthmicks; the great architect and Engineer of the famous and admirable Portable Fabric of Dover Castle, her Ordnance and Artillery, and the true voice of Himself, his Games, Mirth, Fortification".[4]

The "Dover Castle" referred to in Wallington's poem was a moveable wooden structure erected to entertain the crowds during the "Olimpicks" held each year. It was shaped and fashioned like a real castle, even including small cannon which fired blanks. This was a diversion for those who were unable or unwilling to participate in the more strenuous activities included in the Games.[5] To judge by this innovation and by his ability to provide activities for people with varied interests, it seems that

Chapter One: The Olympic Games

Dover possessed the instincts of a true impresario.

Dover's Games flourished for about thirty years, until they were discontinued as a consequence of the turmoil caused by the English Civil War of 1642-1649. They were revived after the restoration of Charles the Second to the English throne and flourished until 1852. After this, they were again abandoned, possibly because they attracted ill-behaved crowds of people from outside the Chipping Campden area. In 1963, the Games were revived for a third time and have continued to be held ever since.

In 2007 the events included: Standing Jump, Putting the Shot, Throwing the Sledge-hammer, Tossing the Caber, a Cross-Country Race and Tugs of War. Perhaps the most bizarre of the events was Shin-Kicking, in which "sport" the contestants held each other by the shoulder and tried to kick each other's shins and to force each other to the ground. The judge for this rather weird event goes under the name of "The Stickler". Part of his job is to ensure that shins are hit before a fall can count.

In recent years the competitors in the Shin-Kicking event have been allowed to protect their shins with straw. It was tougher in the early nineteenth century when the competitors wore boots tipped with iron.

Mr Brookes and Mr Zappas
Where are your Olympic Games? — Panagiotis Soutsos

In 1850, two hundred and thirty-eight years after Robert Dover's Games were first held, an English doctor, William Penny Brookes (1809-1895), organized what he called the "Wenlock Olympic Games" in the small English town of Much Wenlock in the County of Shropshire. It is possible that Brookes knew of the writings of the Greek poet and newspaper publisher, Panagiotis Soutsos. — In 1835, Soutsos had proposed a revival of the Games in his native country. — It is more likely, however, that Brookes was influenced by Joseph Strutt's popular book, *Sports and*

Chapter One: The Olympic Games

Pastimes of the People of England, first published in 1801, which contained references to Robert Dover's Games.[6]

Meanwhile, in Greece, Soutsos' Olympic idea captured the imagination of Evangelis Zappas, a successful businessman. Zappas asked the Greek government to organize a modern Olympics in Athens and offered to meet any expenses that might be incurred. The government was not enthusiastic, despite the offer of financial support. After much negotiation, however, Games were finally staged in Athens in 1859, as part of an agricultural and industrial competition. The prizes included a draft for ten British Pounds contributed by Dr Brookes, as Secretary, on behalf of the Wenlock Olympian Class (one of the classes organized by the Wenlock Agricultural Reading Society, which Dr Brookes had founded). The 1859 Games were taken as the model for Games held in Athens in 1870 and for watered-down versions held in 1875 and 1893.

The Modern Games

Until the early 1980s, based on a record created mainly by himself, Baron Pierre de Coubertin (pronounced "koo-ber-tan"), was given full credit by many (including himself) for reintroducing the Games. (It is now acknowledged among academic sports historians and the sporting community that he was not solely responsible.) A Frenchman, disturbed by the French defeat in the Franco-Prussian War (1870-1871), he felt that the best way to achieve cooperation among the world's nations would be through peaceful international athletic contests. It was his conviction that such contests could bring together the youth of the world in healthy physical activities, irrespective of differences in race, culture or politics.

The Oaths and the Olympic Flag

De Coubertin's philosophy is echoed in the Olympic Oaths. The first of these is taken by a single representative Olympic official

Chapter One: The Olympic Games

on behalf of all judges and officials at the Games:
"In the name of all judges and officials, I promise that we shall officiate in these Olympic Games with complete impartiality, respecting and abiding by the rules which govern them, in the true spirit of sportsmanship."

Similarly, an oath is sworn by one athlete on behalf of all athletes at the Games:
"In the name of all the competitors I promise that we shall take part in these Olympic Games, respecting and abiding by the rules which govern them, committing ourselves to a sport without doping and without drugs, in the true spirit of sportsmanship, for the glory of sport and the honour of our teams."[7]

The Olympic Flag was another innovation. It was flown for the first time as an official symbol in the Olympic Games held in 1920 in Belgium. Its five coloured rings represent the five continents. Today, the "festoon", as it is often called, provides the International Olympic Committee with a substantial income which is derived from selling it to international companies and from fees paid by television companies.

The Charter

De Coubertin's ideas are enshrined today in a Charter of fifty-one chapters and sixty-one articles, linking the Olympic philosophy with ethics and education in the following words:

"Olympism is a philosophy of life, exalting and combining in a balanced whole the qualities of body, will and mind. Blending sport with culture and education, Olympism seeks to create a way of life based on the joy found in effort, the educational value of good example and respect for universal fundamental ethical principles."[8]

These ideals have proved difficult to live up to. Even the Baron himself found this to be true. Anxious to maintain his reputation as the Founder of the revived Olympic movement, he failed to give due recognition to the earlier work of William

Chapter One: The Olympic Games

Brookes in Much Wenlock and Evangelis Zappas in Athens. (He may not have known about Robert Dover in Chipping Campden.)

In 1890, Baron de Coubertin visited Dr Brookes in Much Wenlock. According to David C. Young,[9] Dr Brookes asked the Baron to plant a tree, hoping that the Olympic idea might grow in the same way as the tree. Brookes then showed de Coubertin the victors' list from the 1859 Zappas Olympics and newspaper reports of his own proposals for the introduction of an Olympic Games in Athens. Following that visit, the Wenlock archives record that on Saturday, 25 October 1890, Dr Brookes received a letter from Pierre de Coubertin. The letter thanked Dr Brookes for a photograph sent to him by the Doctor. It enclosed one of his (de Coubertin's) own photographs. In his memoirs, however, de Coubertin makes no mention of the Zappas Olympics or Brookes's Olympic efforts.

Four years after visiting Dr Brookes, de Coubertin formed the International Olympic Committee. Brookes was invited to attend the 1894 "Conference of the Sorbonne" to set up an international Modern Olympic Games, and indeed appears on the list of delegates, but he had broken his leg and was unable to attend.[10] The first modern Games took place in Athens in 1896 but William Brookes did not live to visit them. Unfortunately, he died three months before they took place, aged eighty-six.

The Wenlock Olympian Games are still an annual event. The 121st Games took place from 13 to 16 July 2007. (During and for some years after the First and Second World Wars, no Games were held.) The Wenlock Olympian Games is essentially a Club athletics meeting with competitors from Athletic Clubs across the United Kingdom. The sports include archery, athletics, bowls, clay pigeon shooting, cricket, fencing, five-a-side football, golf, a seven mile road race, tennis, volley ball and a triathlon.

The town of Much Wenlock is an international tourist attraction. Tourists from many different countries doubtless often find their way to the Games as well. And the connection with the

Chapter One: The Olympic Games

International Olympic Games is known.

For example, in 2005, a very moving Torch Lighting ceremony for the Special Olympic Flame of Hope took place in Much Wenlock. This heralded the seventh Special Olympics held (for persons with learning disabilities) in the city of Glasgow, Scotland. Following the ceremony, a team of police officers from across Britain ran with the torch from London to Glasgow. These "Special Games" were the largest sporting event to take place in Great Britain in 2005 and involved 2,800 athletes and over 1,500 volunteers.

Some Key Words

Ancient	Festoon	Sanctuary
Chariot	Pagan	Turmoil
Ethics	Resurrected	

QUIZ
1. When were the ancient Olympic Games revived?
2. Who was Zeus?
3. What was the only sport offered in the ancient, revived Games?
4. What was Pindar famous for?
5. When did the revived ancient Games end?
6. Who banned the ancient Games?
7. Who first proposed the revival of the Games in modern Greece?
8. Where did Dr Brookes live?
9. When were the first modern Olympic Games held in Athens?

"A special or autumn festival in connection with Wenlock Olympian Society was held on Wednesday, under the presidency of Mr R. B. Benson, of Lutwyche Hall. The object of the festival was chiefly to enlighten Baron Pierre de Coubertin, a French gentleman, who desires to introduce athletics more largely amongst his own countrymen, upon the methods adopted for the training of athletes in England. Dr Brookes, who is an untiring advocate of physical education among the young, was on this occasion largely instrumental in bringing about this meeting."[11]

Forward to Beijing! A Guide to the Summer Olympics

Runner J. M. Park proudly holds aloft the Olympic torch on its detour to Hong Kong on the way to the Tokyo Olympics in 1964. *Photo courtesy HKSAR Government.* ~ Dr Park later competed as a yachtsman in the Tokyo Olympics. ~ The first Hong Kong athlete given the honour of carrying the flame was Chung Kin-man, one of the four swimmers who made up Hong Kong's first Olympic team in Helsinki in 1952. For the Beijing Olympics, 19,400 runners will take part in the relay. Eight will be "China-loving expats", chosen following an online campaign in which almost 300,000 people voted.

Chapter Two

THE MODERN OLYMPIC MOVEMENT

Triumphs and Troubles
A spectacular ceremony is held at the opening of each modern Olympic Games. In 2008, there will be a parade of athletes in the Beijing National Stadium. This will be led by the Greek team. The host team will come next and then athletes from all the competing countries will follow and parade round the stadium, clad in immaculate blazers or colourful robes; stimulated by triumphant music but certainly conscious of the television cameras. The Olympic Flag will be raised and the Olympic Anthem will be played. (This Anthem was written for the first modern Games held in 1896 but in subsequent Olympics it was replaced by other compositions until it was re-introduced in 1960. It is now assured of a permanent place as the official anthem.) After the last bars of the Anthem have been sounded, a runner will enter the arena holding the Olympic Torch. This will have been carried from Olympia, Greece, through each of the continents except Antarctica by a relay of over 21,000 runners. Being still alight, it will be used to light a cauldron which will remain lit until it is extinguished in the Closing Ceremony. At the close of the Opening Ceremony, a flock of doves will be released into the air to symbolize the free spirit of the Games.

    The first Hong Kong athlete given the privilege of carrying the flame was Chung Kin-man, one of four swimmers who made up Hong Kong's first Olympic team in Helsinki in 1952. In 1988, Gilbert U King-hung, shooter (interior decorator by profession) carried the flame for 100 metres of the 40 km journey.[12] In 1964, as "strenuously" negotiated by Mr A. de O. Sales,[13] the flame made a detour in Hong Kong on its way to Tokyo and was carried in Hong Kong by a total of fifteen runners.

    Already in the final months of 2007, there was

Chapter Two: The Modern Olympic Movement

considerable interest and discussion of who will carry the flame on its way to the Opening Ceremony of the Beijing Olympics, particularly about those who will carry it on the Mainland of China itself.

The position of final torch-bearer or torch bearers has been coveted since the accolade was first granted to Fritz Schilgen in the Berlin Games of 1936. At certain Games, more than one person has been nominated.

Usually representing the host country, the following athletes have been honoured in this way since the Olympic Games were resumed in 1948:

London 1948	John Mark
Helsinki 1952	Paavo Nurmi
Melbourne 1956	Ron Clarke (Melbourne); Hans Wikne/ Karin Lindberg/ Henry Eriksson (Stockholm)
Rome 1960	Giancarlo Peris
Tokyo 1964	Yoshinori Sakai
Mexico City 1968	Norma Enriqueta Basilio de Sotelo
Munich 1972	Günter Zahn
Montreal 1976	Sandra Henderson and Stéphane Préfontaine
Moscow 1980	Sergey Belov
Los Angeles 1984	Rafer Johnson
Seoul 1988	Son Kee-Chung, Lim Chun-Ae, Chung Sun-Man, Kim Won-Tak, Sohn Mi-Chung
Barcelona 1992	Antonio Rebollo
Atlanta 1996	Muhammad Ali
Sydney 2000	Cathy Freeman
Athens 2004	Nikolaos Kaklamanakis

Chapter Two: The Modern Olympic Movement

Organisation of the Games

The Olympic Movement is led by three organizations: the International Sport Federations (ISFs) the Olympic Games Organizing Committees (OGOCs) and the International Olympic Committee (IOC). The IOC has its headquarters in Lausanne, Switzerland from which base it oversees 186 national Olympic Committees. Its membership includes diplomats and politicians, senior sports administrators and former athletes. Together, these persons elect an Executive Board, presided over by an official with the title of President.

As might be expected, successive organizers of the Games have had to adapt to different circumstances and to the moods of their times. They have been obliged to cope with national rivalries, terrorist murders, violence, use of performance-enhancing drugs and bribery. Audiences have grown from the relatively small number of supporters and officials who attended the first modern Games, to the many thousands who visited the most recent Games and the millions who followed them on television screens, radios and mobile phones.

Kindness and Morality

The Olympic Games have provided opportunities for moments of moral statement and kindness and these have been well documented. Few may now remember the thoughtful action of the Australian rower, Henry Pearce. In the 1928 Games, he stopped rowing to enable a family of ducks to paddle in front of his boat. More will recall the British runner, Eric Liddell, partly because of the well-received film, *Chariots of Fire*, issued some fifty-seven years after the conclusion of the 1924 Games.

The film told the story of the early struggles and eventual victories of the Scotsman Liddell and Harold Abrahams, of Lithuanian Jewish ancestry. Before the Games began, Liddell, a devout Christian, withdrew from both the 100 metre dash and the relays because they were unexpectedly scheduled to take place on

Chapter Two: The Modern Olympic Movement

a Sunday, the Sabbath. Liddell was not the first to withdraw from competition for religious reasons. In the 1900 Games held in Paris, Myer Prinstein, a strict Methodist, opted out of the long jump final held on a Sunday. Despite his absence, he was placed second in the competition because the results from the qualifying rounds were added to the results in the final.

A year after competing in the 1924 Games, Eric Liddell travelled to China where he joined his father as a missionary in Weifang, in Tientsin Province. Japanese troops overran that part of China and Liddell was interned, together with other foreigners. He died in captivity in February 1945 of a brain tumour. The site of the internment camp is now occupied by a school. It was there, forty-five years after his death, that a memorial was dedicated in Liddell's name. The dedication of the memorial coincided with the formation of the Eric Liddell Foundation, set up to promote cross-cultural links among students from China, Hong Kong and Great Britain. A few words from Isaiah are inscribed on the memorial stone:

"They shall mount up with wings as eagles; they shall run and not be weary." (Isaiah 40:31)

Pietri's Consolation
It was the unintended result of a kind action that brought about the disqualification of a gifted marathon runner. In the 1908 race at the London Games, the leader, Dorando Pietri, collapsed four times in the stadium. Recovering somewhat, but still befuddled, he staggered blindly towards the finishing tape. Observing the runner's plight, the stadium announcer helped him to breast the tape. Because he had accepted this assistance, Pietri was disqualified and the gold medal was awarded to an American, Joseph Hayes. On the day after the race, however, Pietri received a gold trophy as a consolation prize. The prize was presented to him personally by Queen Alexandra of England.

Chapter Two: The Modern Olympic Movement

Where Was the Sweetness and Light?
In contrast to these displays of compassion and humanity, political manœuvring has sometimes marred the Olympics. It has been said that Baron de Coubertin was influenced by the writings of Matthew Arnold, the British poet and educationist. But, to use a phrase coined by Arnold, the Games have not always been characterised by their "sweetness and light." National concerns have sometimes taken precedence over the maintenance of harmonious international relations. For example, in the Stockholm Games of 1912, Russia questioned the inclusion of a team entered by Finland, then part of the Russian Empire. Similarly, Austria complained that Bohemia was part of the Austro-Hungarian Empire and therefore could not legitimately enter a team under its own name (as it had done).

Exclusion
The Games scheduled for 1916 did not take place because of the bloody chaos of the First World War. When they were revived again in 1920, lingering political tensions resulted in the exclusion of competitors from Austria, Bulgaria, Germany, Hungary and Turkey. An opportunity for healing was lost. The same countries were excluded again in 1924 when the Games were held in Paris.

Inclusion
In 1928, the Germans and their former allies were allowed to rejoin the Olympic Movement at Amsterdam. This was also the occasion on which Johnny Weissmuller, the handsome Romanian/American swimmer, repeated his triumph in the Paris Games by winning the 100-metre freestyle and the 4 x 200-metre freestyle relay. These triumphs provided a career opportunity. Weissmuller went on to play the part of Tarzan in twelve popular films, based on Edgar Rice Burroughs's novels about a man brought up by apes.

Chapter Two: The Modern Olympic Movement

The Cost of Travel
In Los Angeles in 1932, Paavo Nurmi from Finland was banned on the grounds that he had breached amateur rules by accepted travelling expenses to attend various competitions. The International Olympics Committee's action was deliberate. The mistake made in the 3,000 metre steeplechase was not. Inadvertently, the lap counter added an extra lap to the race. The unfortunate result was that the American, Joseph McCluskey, was overtaken and lost his place in favour of the British runner, Thomas Evenson. Evenson was able to take second place. McCluskey accepted a bronze medal without complaint.

Germany Triumphant (almost)
Politics came right to the fore at the Games held in Berlin in 1936. The German Dictator, Adolph Hitler, seized upon the Games as a perfect opportunity to extol the virtues of the "Aryan race" to the world outside. He had some success, for, despite the triumphs of the black American runner, Jesse Owens, who won four gold medals, Germany was awarded a total of thirty-three gold medals and the German team finished as the overall medal winners in the competition.

Troubles in Mexico
Although not a government body, but rather a non-governmental organization (NGO), the International Olympic Committee took direct political action against South Africa in 1964 by condemning its apartheid policies and banning it from participation in the Tokyo Games. The Committee also withdrew its invitation to South Africa to compete in the 1968 Games. These sanctions remained in place until 1992.

Different issues clouded the Mexico Games, the first being the opposition expressed by many people to the Games, on the grounds that Mexico was a poor country and could not afford them. This opposition turned to violence when approximately ten

Chapter Two: The Modern Olympic Movement

thousand people, including many students, marched to a central square in the city. The government called in the army and shots were fired. Two hundred and sixty people were killed and many hundreds were wounded.

It was at these same Games in Mexico that two American runners, Tommy Smith (gold medal) and John Carlos (bronze medal) appointed themselves as champions of black peoples' rights and Black Power. They demonstrated their support by raising black-gloved fists at the medal-awarding ceremony for the two hundred metre race. Both men were sent back to the United States in disgrace. After they returned to the United States, Smith taught social science and coached athletics at Santa Monica College, California and Carlos was employed as a coach at Palm Springs High School, Florida.

African Boycott
The boycott introduced by the International Olympics Committee in 1964 started a trend. In 1976, 22 African countries opted out of the Games on the grounds that New Zealand's team had played rugby in a South Africa that was still blighted by the policy of apartheid.

America Withdraws: the USSR Persists
This trend continued in 1980 when President Carter of the United States put forward the Russian invasion of Afghanistan as a reason for requesting that the Olympic Games should not be held in Moscow, but in a different location. The United States' Olympic Committee supported Carter's request but the IOC did not. After much political wrangling, the Games went ahead in Moscow as planned, despite being boycotted by the United States and other national teams. The British Olympic Association sent teams to Moscow and was one of a number of Associations that defied their governments' requests. In trade union terms, these Associations might have been dubbed "blacklegs".

Chapter Two: The Modern Olympic Movement

The USSR Withdraws: America Persists
Continuing the international game of "tit for tat", the Soviet Union decided to absent itself from the 1984 Games in Los Angeles. Thirteen other countries supported the Soviet action and did not appear.

China Resurgent
On a more positive note, China took part in the Los Angeles Games, a significant addition after an absence of thirty-two years. The time between Games had not been wasted. Chinese athletes won fifteen gold medals, eight silver medals and nine bronze medals. The country took fourth place in the final rankings.

Further Violence
The violence experienced in Mexico in 1968 gave way to further violence at the Munich Games of 1972. The current situation in the Middle East is a constant reminder of the attack on members of the Israeli team which resulted in the deaths of eleven athletes, five terrorists and one policeman.

Following the Munich incident, reinforced security measures at all the Games, held between 1972 and 1996, failed to stop a terrorist in 1996 from exploding a bomb in the middle of a music concert in Atlanta's new Centennial Olympic Park, so named after the Olympic Games that were revived a hundred years earlier, in 1896. Richard Jewell, a security guard who was accused of planning the attack was later found to be innocent and was cleared of all charges. He was later honoured for moving people out of harm's way. He died in 2007. The real bomber, one Eric Rudolph, was arrested and pleaded guilty. He is now serving a life sentence in prison.

Drugs for the Dopes
The first instance of a drug being used to bolster performance — and perhaps survival — occurred in the Saint Louis Games of

Chapter Two: The Modern Olympic Movement

1904. The winner of the marathon, Thomas Hicks, finished the race with the help of a draft of strychnine sulfate, given to him by his coach, ten miles before the finishing line. No action was taken against Hicks, although Albert Coray (who came second) of France, and Arthur Newton of the United States (who came third) had just cause to complain.

Drugs may have been used to enhance performance at the Olympic Games before 1968 but this was the year that IOC suspicions were brought out into the open. For the first time, the Committee ordered drug tests to be carried out after each competition. This action proved to be appropriate for in 1988, in a much-publicised case, the Canadian sprinter, Ben Johnson, was found to have taken a performance-enhancing substance. This, it seems, helped him to become, if only briefly, "the fastest man in the world".

After 1968, a second Olympic competition began, not only on the running track, but between certain athletes and the Committee's medical advisers. As investigative procedures improve, however, drug takers may now be exposed much earlier than in the past. At the year 2000 Sydney Games, the investigators were clearly on their toes. They banned no fewer than thirty-five athletes for failing drugs tests after the appropriate procedures had been implemented.

Unpleasant Flavours at Salt Lake
At the Winter Games, held in Salt Lake City in 2002, a number of athletes were found to have taken drugs. On the last day alone, three cross-country skiers were disqualified after being found to have ingested a drug named Darbepoetin.

Drug abuse was not the only scandal to cast a shadow over the Salt Lake City Games and the competitors were not the sole culprits. The Canadians performed very well in the pairs figure skating finals but Russia was awarded the gold medal. After an enquiry, it was established that a French judge had been

Chapter Two: The Modern Olympic Movement

persuaded to vote in Russia's favour. To settle the matter, both Russia and Canada were presented with gold medals.

Such was the shocking behaviour at Salt Lake City that the Games were dubbed "Skategate" in the popular press. This was a reference to the "Watergate" scandal that affected the United States in the Seventies and which led eventually to the resignation of President Richard Nixon in August 1974. The Watergate is a luxurious hotel and residential complex that was the scene of a break-in by men employed by factions of the Republican political party. Their aim was to photograph documents in the offices of the Democratic Party's National Committee. The burglars were, however, discovered. The result was that the President (a Republican) was discredited.

Restoring Order

Despite the high ideals of the modern founders — Dover, Brookes, Zappas and de Coubertin — and the courage, determination and honest efforts of many competitors, the Olympic Games had for many years been affected by political strife, boycotts, violence and drug abuse. In 1999, the IOC bowed to the inevitable and recognized, perhaps belatedly, that the time had come to restore order. The participants, whether competitors, coaches, judges, administrators, or those involved in the bidding processes, could not be relied upon to discipline themselves or to respect the Olympic Charter, which aims, "to create a way of life based on the joy found in effort, the educational value of good example and respect for universal fundamental ethical principles".

Accordingly, the Committee decided to establish an Ethics Commission with the following Terms of Reference:

To develop and update a framework of ethical principles, including a Code of Ethics, based upon the values and principles enshrined in the Olympic Charter.

To develop and promote best practice in the application of the ethical principles and suggest concrete measures to this end.

Chapter Two: The Modern Olympic Movement

To provide assistance, including advice, upon request by the IOC, to the cities wishing to organize the Olympic Games, in order that the ethical principles are applied in practice.

To help ensure compliance with the ethical principles in the policies and practices of the IOC , the cities wishing to organize the Olympic Games, the NOCs, the OCOGs and the participants within the framework of the Olympic Games.

To assess the extent to which ethical principles are being reflected in practice.

To investigate complaints raised in relation to the non-respect of the ethical principles, including breaches of the Code of Ethics, and if necessary propose sanctions to the Executive Board.

To review guidelines within the IOC as to how they relate to the ethical principles, in particular the guidelines applicable to cities wishing to organize the Olympic Games, and to make comments and/or recommendations related thereto.

On 26 April 2007 in Beijing, the IOC Executive Board adopted a Code of Ethics that focuses on the Dignity and Integrity of the Games as well as on Resources, Candidatures, Relations with States and Confidentiality.

The preamble to the Code states that "The International Olympic Committee and each of its members, the cities wishing to organise the Olympic Games, the Organizing Committees of the Olympic Games and the National Olympic Committees (hereinafter "the Olympic parties") restate their commitment to the Olympic Charter and in particular its Fundamental Principles. The Olympic parties affirm their loyalty to the Olympic ideal inspired by Pierre de Coubertin. Consequently at all times the Olympic parties and, in the framework of the Olympic Games, the participants, undertake to respect and ensure respect of the present Code."

Chapter Two: The Modern Olympic Movement

The Winter Games

Following long-established custom, the Summer Olympic Games have been held every four years since 1896, except for the war years 1916, 1940 and 1944. Games appropriate for the winter season were ignored until, in 1922, the French Olympic Committee organized a Winter Sports Week in Chamonix. The event was declared to be successful by the sixteen participating countries, despite hostile weather conditions. Enthused by this "trial run", the IOPC decided to organize Winter Games every four years, at first in the same years as the Summer Games.

From the Olympics to Hollywood
In 1928, the first full Winter Games were held in the Swiss resort of St. Moritz. The programme included cross-country skiing, bob-sledding, ice hockey and figure-skating. The latter event launched Sonja Henie, a young figure-skater from Norway, on a Hollywood film career, a success story similar to that enjoyed by the swimmer, Johnny Weissmuller, following the Summer Games held in the same year, 1928.

Overcoming Depression
Both the Summer Games and the Winter Games of 1932 were held during the worldwide Depression. The 1932 Games took place in the Adirondack Mountains in New York State. In contrast to the twenty-five countries that took part in St. Moritz in 1938, only seventeen nations could afford to compete in 1932. The Games did, however, manage to overcome warm weather problems — the ice turned to slush — and gave the maturing Sonja Henie another opportunity to repeat her triumph of 1928. Her free programme included extracts from popular stage musicals and this may have influenced the Hollywood talent scouts who later recommended that she be launched on a film career.
  The Winter Games of 1936, held in Germany's Garmisch-

Chapter Two: The Modern Olympic Movement

Partenkirchen, were not held at the best of times, nor in the friendliest country. For Nazi Germany was flexing its muscles, preparing for the worldwide conflict that was to begin three years later. Ironically, it took second place in the final medals list to Norway, a country that it would invade and occupy from 1940 to 1945. In the 1936 Summer Games that followed, Germany had greater medals success.

Post War Manoeuvres

At the time of the 1948 Winter Games Germany had been defeated but the organizers had to deal with a controversy that seemed to be very important at the time. This related to the American decision to send two different ice hockey teams, one nominated by the US National Olympic Committee and the other by the Amateur Hockey Association of the United States. Although the Association's team enjoyed itself thoroughly and finished in fourth place, it was disqualified, after much deliberation, a year later.

The 1952 Winter Games were held in Oslo, seven years after the end of the Second World War. With grace and friendliness, the Norwegians received de-nazified athletes from Germany, the country that had occupied their own for nearly six years. The renegade Norwegian army officer, Vidkun Quisling, was already a forgotten man, although not in his own country. Following the invasion and occupation of Norway by the Germans, Quisling was appointed to the post of "Minister President", by a Nazi official. He cooperated to the full with the Nazis, doing nothing, for example, to prevent the shipment of Norwegian Jews to concentration camps in Germany and elsewhere. Executed by firing squad at the end of the War, his name has become a synonym for "betrayer."

West or East?

"Glasnost" for Germany seemed almost to be possible when, at

Chapter Two: The Modern Olympic Movement

the 1956 Cortina d'Ampezzo Games, a pan-German team competed. Accommodating German competitors at the 1960 Winter Games in Squaw Valley, Sierra Nevada, proved more of a problem, since the pan-German team wished to display two different flags, one for East Germany and the other for West Germany. Each "country" wished its athletes to bear its own flag at the opening ceremony which was orchestrated by Walt Disney as efficiently as the activities that now take place daily in the various "theme parks" which bear his name

After much discussion, a compromise was reached and a single flag was used by both German teams, a flag that bore the national colours of Germany, together with the five Olympic rings.

Bring on More Snow!
In 1964, the organizers of the Winter Games at Innsbruck had to deal with a familiar problem, a shortage of snow. They solved it by engaging Austrian soldiers to transport huge quantities of snow to the competition fields and valleys.

At Grenoble in 1968, the German question came up again, no doubt to the irritation of the organizers. On this occasion, two German teams paraded around the stadium. Both, however, bore the same flag and ambled around to the same music by Beethoven.

No German "incidents" coloured the 1972 Games, organised by Germany's wartime ally, Japan, in Sapporo, the largest city in cold Hokkaido. There were few matters of controversy, except that a competitor from Austria was made to withdraw on the grounds that he had offended against the IOC's amateur regulations.

The 1976 Winter Games were held in Innsbruck for the second time. There the USSR team completely outdistanced other countries, gaining a total of thirteen gold, six silver and eight bronze medals.

Chapter Two: The Modern Olympic Movement

No Snow? We'll make our own!
It was obviously easier for the IOC to consider bids for the Summer Games than for the Winter Games, since the latter depended so much upon the elements. As seemed to be usual at the New York resort of Lake Placid, there was a shortage of snow. This handicap was overcome by the use of artificial snow for the first time.

The 1980 Summer Games in Moscow came to a satisfactory end, despite being boycotted by the United States and allies such as Japan and West Germany. It was, therefore, no surprise when the USSR collected eighty gold medals, East Germany forty-seven medals and Bulgaria, Cuba and Italy eight gold medals each. The USSR was the overall winner with a total of one hundred and ninety-five gold, silver and bronze medals.

Sarajevo! The word conjures up the names of Bosnia-Herzegovina and Kosevo, and images of bloody conflict between Serbs, Croats and Albanians. In 1984, there were political rumblings beneath the surface but there they remained while the Games proceeded. At the conclusion, the East Germans topped the medal bill with nine gold medals and the USSR came second, with six golds. Despite the perfect scores gained by the elegant British ice dancers, Jayne Torvill and Christopher Dean, Britain's haul of medals was very small.

At Calgary in 1988, the Winter Games included, for the first time, crowd-pleasing demonstration events such as freestyle skiing, short track speed skating and curling. At the same Games, disabled athletes competed against each other, with their own timetable of events.

Germany United?
In 1992, France played host at Albertville to Games which reflected the significant political changes that had taken place since the Games of 1988. Newly-independent Lithuania, Latvia and Estonia flew their own flags and Germany competed as a

Chapter Two: The Modern Olympic Movement

reunited country and took home the most medals, a nice collection of ten gold, ten silver and six bronze.

The next Winter Games took place two years after those held in Albertville. The IOC had decided that from 1994, and onwards the Summer and Winter Games would be held alternately every two years. The introduction of this new timetable meant that the organizers in the Norwegian town of Lillehammer had a shorter time than usual in which to prepare. Nevertheless, the events were very successful and the hosts welcomed South Africa after a thirty-four-year absence, as well as teams from the independent republics of Georgia, Russia, Ukraine and from war-torn Bosnia-Herzegovina, also an independent republic.

Memories of the Ice Palace and the 1972 Games in Sapporo were still fresh in some veteran athletes' minds when the 1998 Games were staged in Nagano on the island of Honshu in Japan. Seventy-two countries took part in the Games. Germany topped the medal bill with twelve gold, nine silver and eight bronze medals.

The athletes banned for drug abuse in the 2002 Winter Games in Salt Lake City committed the offences knowing that, whilst certainly they were guilty of offences against the Olympic Code, the judges also could not be trusted, in particular the judge of the figure skating pairs competition who wilted under pressure and cast his vote in favour of Russia, as mentioned above. A fine event in an excellent setting was spoilt by the dishonest actions of the few.

In the year 2006, the Winter Sports were held for the first time in Torino in Italy. The Games lasted for seventeen days and took place at six different sites, all situated in the Italian Alps. The events that brought disgrace to Salt Lake City were not repeated in hospitable Italy.

Chapter Two: The Modern Olympic Movement

Some Key Words and Phrases

Befuddled
Bob-sledding
Boycott
Chaos
Consolation
Cross-cultural
Denazified
Extol

Factions
Flexing
"Glasnost"
International Olympic
Committee (IOC)
Internment
Resurgent
Slush

QUIZ
1. Where does the International Olympic Committee have its headquarters?
2. What was Henry Pearce's thoughtful action?
3. What does the motto, "Citius, Altius, Fortius", mean?
4. What were the names of the two principal characters in the film, "Chariots of Fire"?
5. Why was Dorando Pietri disqualified?
6. What British writer influenced Baron de Coubertin?
7. Why were the 1916 Olympic Games cancelled?
8. What part did Johnny Weissmuller play in several films?
9. Why was Paavo Nurmi forbidden to enter for the Los Angeles Games in 1932?
10. What was the name of the black runner who disappointed Adolf Hitler in the 1936 Games?
11. Why did many people in Mexico oppose the Olympic Games in 1968?
12. Why did a large number of African countries withdraw from the 1976 Olympic Games?
13. Why did the USA not participate in the 1980 Olympiad?
14. What important country took part in the 1984 Games after a long absence?
15. What is the name of the "fastest man in the world", who was disqualified in 1988.

Preview Ceremony of "2004 Olympic Games" Stamp Sheetlet. Mr Allan CHIANG, Postmaster General, Hong Kong & Mr Timothy FOK. *Photo Courtesy SFOCHKC.* ~ Many countries issue special stamps to celebrate the Olympics. Hong Kong's first were in 1992. Also in 1992, the Hong Kong Post co-sponsored the 1992 Olympic Games (with thirty other Postal Authorities, each serving as official express courier for the Games within their own country or territory).[14]

Athens 2004 The Games of the XXVIII Olympiad: Flag Presentation Ceremony, Hong Kong, SAR, China. Among many senior figures, the group includes then Hong Kong Chief Executive the Hon. Mr TUNG Chee Wah, The Hon. Timothy FOK Tsun Ting and The Hon. Arnaldo de Oliveira SALES. *Photo Courtesy SFOCHKC.*

Chapter Three

1896-1984

Some Highlights

Athletes from thirteen countries participated in the first modern Games held in Greece in April, 1896. Nine different sports featuring forty-two events were included in the programme. Two hundred and forty-five athletes competed in these events. In contrast, more than ten thousand competitors took part in over two hundred and seventy events in the 2004 Games held in the same country, Greece, mainly in Athens.

Each of the sports included in the modern Summer Olympic Games has a different history. Some sports have remained unchanged in the programme from 1896. Others have been added, modified or discontinued as the years have gone by. The following are selected highlights of the Games that took place from 1896 to 1984.

1896: A Royal Welcome
Greece is now a republic but, in 1896, it was still a monarchy. It was therefore fitting that the first modern Games should be declared open by the King of Greece, George I. Crown Prince Constantine, later King Constantine, gave a welcoming speech.

Starting as they meant to continue in all Olympic Competitions, American athletes were very successful at the first of the modern Games, winning eleven gold medals to Greece's ten.

The first sports postage stamps were issued to celebrate the revived Games.

Leon Pyrgos, a Greek Fencer, was the first Greek winner of the Fencing Masters Foil event. This event has been discontinued. Other Greek athletes to distinguish themselves in

Chapter Three: 1896-1984: Some Highlights

1896 were Louis Spyridon in the Marathon, Ionnis Georgiadis in the individual sabre competition and Pantelis Karasevdas in the Free Rifle Shooting event.

Paris: 1900

French athletes dominated the 1900 Games, earning twenty-nine medals, no doubt to the satisfaction of the French founder of the modern Games, Baron de Courbertin.

Unfortunately, the Olympics received relatively little support from the public. They were overshadowed by the Exposition Universelle Internationale, the World Fair.

So little exposure was there that it has been said that up to their death many participants died without realizing that they had taken part in the Olympics.

St. Louis: 1904

The St. Louis Games were held over a period of some five months, from July until November. They aroused relatively little interest.

An American marathon competitor attracted some attention by seeking and enjoying a lift on the way to the finishing line. Needless to say, he was disqualified.

London: 1908

Britain organized the 1908 Games at very short notice after Italy withdrew its bid for economic and other reasons. Mount Vesuvius had erupted in 1906, causing the death of over a hundred people. This was the worst eruption to take place since Pompeii and Herculaneum were buried under molten lava in AD 79.

At the start of the Games, the athletes paraded behind their national flags. They were not, however, clad in the smart uniforms that we have seen in recent times. Neither were they taking photographs of the crowd and other athletes with digital cameras!

Chapter Three: 1896-1984: Some Highlights

This was the Olympics in which, as mentioned earlier, the leader in the marathon, Dorando Pietri, collapsed on the track. He was helped over the line by officials and consequently was disqualified.

Stockholm: 1912

An enthusiastic reception was given to the 1912 Games in Stockholm. Two American athletes distinguished themselves. Duke Paoa Kahanamoku, an Hawaiian, won three gold and two silver medals in swimming. Hawaii's benevolent climate gave Kahanamoku the opportunity to practice in open waters, as well as in land-based pools. Said to have introduced the crawl stroke to the United States, his feat is still spoken of with admiration in present day Hawaii.

In athletics, the Native American, Jim Thorpe, stood out by winning both the pentathlon and the decathlon. After the Games were over however, Thorpe was deprived of his medals on the grounds that he had received payment as a youth for playing professional baseball. The medals were restored and presented to his family in 1983 but Thorpe had died thirty years earlier without satisfaction.

1916

The Games that would normally have taken place in this year did not do so. Many European nations were competing in the grimmer arena of the First World War.

Antwerp: 1920

A Belgian fencer, Victor Boin, was the first Olympic competitor to take the Olympic Oath and the Olympic flag was flown for the first time as the official symbol of the Olympic Games.

The Finnish athlete, Paavo Nurmi, won three gold medals and one silver medal.

Chapter Three: 1896-1984: Some Highlights

Paris: 1924
Building on his successes in the Antwerp Games, Paavo Nurmi earned five gold medals. It was at these Games that Eric Liddell and Harold Abrahams distinguished themselves for Great Britain in the 400m and 100m races respectively.

The Olympic motto Citius, Altius, Fortius (Swifter, Higher, Stronger) was introduced.

Gertrude Ederle won a bronze medal in the 100m freestyle swimming race. Two years later, she swam the British Channel, two hours faster than any man had achieved up to that time.

Despite some distortion and wavering reception, it became possible, for the first time, to listen to a commentary on the Olympic Games, received from a crystal radio set.

Amersterdam: 1928
Paavo Nurmi appeared on the Olympic stage for the third time and won three gold medals. Another alumnus from the Paris Games, Johnny Weissmuller, achieved gold in the 100m freestyle and the 4 x 200m relay in the swimming events. Soon he would achieve success in Hollywood, but not for swimming.

1932: Los Angeles
Mildred "Babe" Didrikson established her reputation as a fine athlete at these games, winning gold medals in the 80m hurdles and the javelin. After giving up her running at Olympic level, she turned to golf and became a champion in that sport, as well.

1936: Berlin
The German dictator, Adolf Hitler, left the Games a disappointed and irritated man. Black athletes from the United State had challenged his views about the superiority of the "Aryan race." The black runner, Jesse Owens, won gold medals for the 100metres and 200metres races, the long jump and the 4 x 100m relay. Hitler should have taken comfort from the fact that

32   Forward to Beijing! A Guide to the Summer Olympics

Chapter Three: 1896-1984: Some Highlights

Germany gained the most number of medals overall (thirty-three).

1940
Once again, the European nations were engaged in another competition. On this occasion, it was the second year of the Second World War.

1944
The Second World War still continued and no Games were possible.

London: 1948
Many of the athletes were obliged to bring their own food to London since war-time rationing was still in force .The "flying housewife" from the Netherlands, the runner Fanny Blankers-Koen, won four gold medals.

For economic reasons, it proved impossible for Britain to build an Olympic Village and the athletes were therefore accommodated in military barracks and colleges close to London.

Helsinki: 1952
Emil Zatopek of Czechoslovakia triumphed in the 5,000m, the 10,000m and the marathon. His wife, Dana, took gold in the women's javelin.

South Korea participated in the Games as a country in its own right.

Melbourne: 1956
Betty Cuthbert of Australia won three gold medals in the 100m, 200m and 4 x 100m relay. She was "outmedalled" by the Soviet gymnast, Larissa Latynina who won four gold medals. At these Olympics, the Australian swimmer, Dawn Fraser, demonstrated her ability at this level, winning two gold medals and one silver.

Chapter Three: 1896-1984: Some Highlights

Rome: 1960
The opening ceremony was characterized for the first time by a parade of the athletes. The Games were accorded widespread television coverage.
 Larissa Latynina of the Soviet Union won three gold medals, two silver medals and one bronze medal, all for gymnastics. Also in gymnastics, her compatriot Boris Shakhlin took home four gold medals, two silver and a bronze.

Tokyo: 1964
Volleyball and Judo were added to the Olympic programme for the first time. In her third Olympics, the Australian, Dawn Fraser, set a new Olympic record in the 100m freestyle swimming event. Don Schollander of the United States of America won four gold medals in the men's swimming competition.

Mexico City: 1968
These were troubled times, with the spread of the so-called drug culture, a bitter war in Vietnam and protests in Mexico about the money spent on the Games. The US sprinters Tommie Smith and John Carlos tried to make a point at a medals ceremony by raising black-gloved fists as symbols of the black power movement.

Munich: 1972
In Mexico City, people protesting against the Games were killed in the streets. In Munich the violence continued. Five terrorists, eleven athletes and a policeman were killed within the Olympic Village itself. On a lighter note, Mark Spitz, the American swimmer, won seven gold medals.

Montreal: 1976
The Olympic flame was lit at all Olympic venues. The first women's basketball tournament took place at these Games. The Soviet team won the gold medal. Kornelia Ender of East Germany

Chapter Three: 1896-1984: Some Highlights

earned four gold medals and a silver medal in the swimming pool. The Soviet Union's Nikolai Andrianov won four gold medals, a silver medal and a bronze medal, all for gymnastics. Nadia Comaneci of Romania delighted spectators with her charm and athletic prowess in the same event, taking home two gold medals, a silver medal and a bronze.

Moscow: 1980
These Games proved to be unique in that thirty-six world records, thirty-nine European records and seventy-three Olympic records were gained. For Great Britain, Steve Ovett and Sebastian Coe (now Lord Coe) continued their friendly rivalry on the running track. Ovett was successful in the 800m race and Coe took first place in the 1,500m event.

Los Angeles: 1984
The sprinter, Carl Lewis, earned four gold medals for the United States. Sebastian Coe successfully defended his 1,500m title and Daley Thompson retained the decathlon title he won in Moscow. Women's synchronized swimming appeared on the Olympic programme for the first time.

QUIZ
1. Who gave the welcoming speech at the opening of the first modern Olympic Games?
2. For what achievement is Gertrude Ederle known, in addition to her success at the Olympics?
3. Why did Great Britain not build an Olympic Village in 1948?
4. In what sport did Mildred Didrikson excel after she ceased to be an Olympic competitor?
5. When did Judo become an Olympic sport?

LEUNG Chun Wai (R1); LAU Yu Leong (R2). Asian Games, 1-15 December 2007, held in Doha, the capital of Qatar, United Arab Emirates. *Photo Courtesy SFOCHKC.*

Hannah WILSON, Aquatics, Athens Summer Olympic Games, 2004.
Photo Courtesy SFOCHKC. ~ Hannah beat her own Hong Kong Women's 100m free-style record with a time of 57.33 seconds.

Chapter Four: Aquatics to Athletics

1988 to 2008

Chapter Four

AQUATICS TO ATHLETICS

Aquatics (sports played on or in water): a long history
Swimming was the only aquatic sport included in the first modern Summer Games held in 1896. Conditions then were much tougher for the competitors than they are today. The contest took place in the Mediterranean Ocean, rather than in an indoor or outdoor swimming pool. Despite its inviting, sparkling blue colour, the ocean water was so cold that Alfred Hajos, the winner of both the 100m freestyle and the 1200m freestyle races, confessed that he was more concerned about survival than the result of the race. Hajos completed the 100m race in 1:22.20 minutes, in sharp contrast to Pieter van den Hoogenband's time of 48.17 seconds, achieved in the Athens Games in 2004.

At the Paris Olympics in 1900, the swimming competition took place in the River Seine. In St Louis, in 1904, competitors were obliged to swim in a small lake. The 1900 Paris Summer Games featured backstroke, team swimming, underwater swimming and obstacle events. Water polo was included in the same year and has remained in the programme ever since. In 1904, the obstacle and underwater swimming events disappeared, but breaststroke, a relay (4 x 50 yards), highboard diving and "Plunge for Distance" were added. In the latter event, the competitors had to dive under the water and (if they could) remain there for sixty seconds before emerging.

The Need for Improvement
Clearly, conditions needed to be improved and more thought given to which aquatics' events were sensible and which were not. With this in mind, representatives from eight participating

Chapter Four: Aquatics to Athletics

countries met a few days after the Summer Olympic Games' opening ceremony in 1908, to draw up rules and devise a more coherent programme for the aquatic events. A start was made in the same year when the swimming competition was narrowed down to freestyle and backstroke racing, a relay (4 x 200m), diving, highboard diving and water polo.

Drawing on experience gained in 1908, a model was established in Stockholm in 1912 for the Olympic aquatics programme. In that year, the men's competition consisted of three freestyle races (100m, 400m and 1,500m), one freestyle relay (4x200m), two breaststroke races, springboard, highboard diving, plain high diving and water polo. For the first time, events were added for women, namely, a 100m freestyle race, a 4x100m relay and highboard diving.

Today, the Summer Games offer twenty-one different swimming events for men. These include springboard platform diving, synchronized springboard diving, platform diving and water polo. There are twenty-two events for women, one more than for men. The women's programme now includes a graceful synchronized swimming duet and a "performance" by a synchronized swimming team. Synchronised diving (diving in pairs) was introduced for the first time in Sydney. The role of women in the Summer Olympics Games was given a boost when women's water polo was added to the programme.

More than just a swimming pool
A nation that hosts the Summer Olympic Games has the opportunity to design new facilities for aquatic sports. These designs must observe the regulations, for example, pools must be 50m long. They must also serve not only the Olympic athletes but also members of the public after the Games have come to an end.

In Athens, the new Aquatic Centre featured two outdoor pools and one indoor pool. In Beijing, a National Swimming Centre has been constructed. Dubbed the "Water Cube" because

Chapter Four: Aquatics to Athletics

of its unique "bubble" appearance, the Centre boasts five pools, a wave machine with rides and a large restaurant. A major recreational asset has been created for use at and beyond the Games.

Testing for drugs
At Seoul in 1988, Kristin Otto from Leipzig was declared by many to be the most successful athlete at the Games, at least for swimming. She won six gold medals, two freestyle races (50m and 100m), the 100m backstroke and the 100m butterfly race. With fellow team members she was awarded two more gold medals in the freestyle and medley team races.

Unfortunately, Otto's reputation has since been marred by the revelation in 1994 that she was given performance-enhancing drugs during her entire career as a swimmer. She was not alone. A number of athletes from former East Germany have now taken legal action against the German government, alleging that the drugs that they were given, when young Olympic aspirants, have been the cause of the serious health problems (including cancer) which many have suffered in recent years.

Drug testing is now a routine practice for all Olympic sports. In the case of swimming, it has so far been done on a random basis.

Useful Terms: Swimming

Backstroke	The swimmer lifts his/her arms out of the water in a circular, backward motion while extending his/her legs in a kicking action.
Breaststroke	The swimmer swims on the breast by extending his/her arms forward and sweeping them back in unison (together).
Butterfly	The swimmer raises both arms and lifts them forwards together.

Chapter Four: Aquatics to Athletics

Freestyle	The swimmer may use any kind of stroke.
Lane	The area of the pool where each swimmer competes during a race.
Lap	One length from one side of the pool to the other.
Synchronised Swimming	In time to music, the competitors make coordinated arm and leg movements in the water.
Flip	To turn over.
Touch	Touching the end of the pool with the hand or hands, completing an event or relay segment.
Tumble turn	An underwater roll at the end of a lap used in backstroke and freestyle swimming, allowing the swimmer to push off from the end of the pool with his or her feet.

The Rules of the Game: Swimming

Olympic competition rules regulate the way synchronised swimming movements and the four strokes, freestyle, butterfly, backstroke and breaststroke, are performed. These rules relate to arm and leg movements, starts, turns, and the length of time swimmers may remain under water.

Each competitor in each different Olympic race must swim a preliminary round. Those swimmers with the sixteen fastest times qualify for the semi-finals in events shorter than 400m. If the event is 400m or longer, or if it is a relay race, the athletes with the eight fastest times go straight into the final.

Lane Allocation
The allocation of swimming lanes is made according to qualifying times. The swimmer with the fastest qualifying time is allocated lane four, the swimmer with the second-fastest time, lane five and so on. The slowest finalist is given lane eight. The middle four

Chapter Four: Aquatics to Athletics

lanes have a slight advantage because there is somewhat less water turbulence. Such turbulence may slow down a competitor. First false starts are ignored but any subsequent false starts lead to disqualification.

Five Styles
In freestyle races, some part of the competitor's body must touch the wall of the pool at the end of each lap and at the finish.
   At the beginning of backstroke events, the swimmers must face the wall with their feet under water. Once the race has started, the competitors must remain under water for the first 15m. Flip turns are allowed when the swimmers reach the walls at each end of the pool.
   In the breaststroke, arm and leg movements must be made together. Only "frog-leg" kicks are allowed to propel the body and part of the head must appear above the surface as each stroke and kick is made. Both hands must touch the walls at the end of each length.
   In the butterfly, competitors are not allowed to swim under water, except for the first stroke and at turns. The swimmers may move their arms above the water and kick their feet and legs up and down.
   In the synchronised swimming event, twenty-four pairs of swimmers participate in a duet competition. Each couple must perform a technical routine of up to two minutes 20 seconds and follow this with a free routine of up to three minutes 30 seconds. The top ten pairs are eligible for the final where they repeat their free routine.

Judging Synchronised Swimming
Swimmers from eight countries go straight into a final in the team event in which they perform a technical routine of two minutes 50 seconds and a free routine of four minutes. Fifty percent of the total marks are awarded for the free routine and fifty percent for

the technical routine. Five judges mark for artistry and five judges mark for technical expertise. Scores for the technical routines are based on three criteria: the difficulty of figures and strokes (30 percent for teams and 40 percent for duets), the ways in which figures and strokes are performed (40 percent) and determining how successful the synchronization is with the music, and within each team (30 percent for teams and 20 percent for duets). As for the free routines, scores are awarded based on three different criteria: according to the manner of presentation, interpretation of the music, and the choreography.

The final scores for each of the routines are obtained by averaging the remaining scores, after the highest and lowest scores have been dropped.

Diving

Diving was first admitted to the Olympic programme in 1904 with 10m platform diving and a "Plunge for Distance", the meaning of which is self-evident. In 1908, a three metre springboard event replaced "Plunge for Distance." Synchronised diving events and diving in pairs were introduced at the Sydney Games in the year 2000.

Useful Terms: Diving

Free	Different positions used in twisting dives.
Pike	The diver bends his/her body at the waist, keeping the legs straight.
Straight	The diver's body remains straight.
Tuck	The diver must bend his/her body at the knees and hips and hold the knees together against the chest.
Entry	The end of a dive counted from the time the competitor enters the water.
Pliable board	A board that can bend easily without breaking.

Chapter Four: Aquatics to Athletics

Synchronised diving
: Two divers mirror each other's height, distance from the springboard or platform, speed of rotation and entry into the water.

Approach
: The forward steps taken by a diver towards the end of the platform or springboard.

The Rules of the Game: Diving

Diving styles include front, back, reverse, inward, twist and arm stand. Points are awarded according to grace and technique. Judges consider the starting position, the run, the take-off, the flights and the entry (which should, if possible, be perpendicular).

Springboard (Men)
The springboard diving competition starts with a preliminary round. The top eight divers move on to a semi-final (five dives) and the top twelve semi-finalists proceed to the final (six dives). The semi-final and final scores are added together to produce a final score. The scores of seven judges are multiplied by coefficients derived from the assumed difficulty of each dive, for example, the most difficult dive (a reverse one-and-a-half somersault with four-and-a-half twists) has a coefficient of 3.7. The easiest dive, a simple forward dive in the tuck position, has a coefficient of 1.2. The athletes jump from a 4.8m long and half-a-metre wide board, set 3m above the water.

Springboard (Women)
As is the case in the men's event, the springboard must be set 3m above the water. Four dives must be performed in the semi-final but the degree of difficulty must not exceed 9.5. Twelve finalists perform five more dives at any degree of difficulty.

Platform and Synchronised Platform (Men)
The platform is a rigid structure, set 10m above the pool. The platform must be at least 6m long and 2m wide. In the Olympic

Chapter Four: Aquatics to Athletics

competition, the semi-finalists dive four times and the finalists dive six times.

Platform and Synchronised Platform (Women)
The platform is the same as that used by the male competitors, that is, it must be constructed 10m above the water as a rigid structure. Semi-finalists have four dives not exceeding 7.6m in difficulty and finalists perform five dives with no limit to the degree of difficulty.

Synchronised Springboard (Men)
Eight pairs of divers compete in this event. Five judges consider the quality of the synchronization and four judges assess the execution of the dives. The lowest and highest scores for both execution and synchronization are abandoned. The remaining scores are then added and multiplied according to the degree of difficulty.

Synchronised Springboard (Women)
There are five rounds in this event.

Water Polo
Water polo was known originally as "football in water" and there is some similarity. The object of the game is to propel a rubber ball into the opposing team's goal. But there the similarity ends. For the goal posts are at the ends of a swimming pool, rather than a field ("pitch").

Useful Terms: Water Polo

Polo	The name given to the rubber ball used when the sport first became popular.
Exclusion foul	A foul that results in a player being sent to an exclusion area for twenty seconds because of unsportsmanlike behaviour.

Chapter Four: Aquatics to Athletics

Penalty foul	A foul that is committed by a defender within a line of four metres from goal. The result is the award of a penalty throw to the opposite team.

The Rules of the Game: Water Polo

An area of 30m in length and 20m in width is marked out for this competition. Each game in the competition lasts for twenty-eight minutes playing time and the competition comprises four seven-minute quarters. Goal posts are erected at each end of the chosen pool. These posts must be three metres apart from each other and their crossbars must be ninety centimeters above the water. The water in the pool must be at least 1.8m deep, with a temperature of between twenty-five degrees and twenty-seven degrees Centigrade.

There are seven players on each team, including the goalkeeper. These players may use any part of the body to score a goal, except a clenched fist. If the team in possession fails to shoot at the goal within thirty-five seconds, then the opposing team takes possession.

In the men's event, twelve teams take part. Four of these teams move up to the quarter finals.

Six women's teams (beginning in the 2000 Olympics) play a round robin round. The top four advance to the semi-finals.

In this quite violent sport, the rules governing fouls are quite complicated, for example, an exclusion foul includes splashing water in an opponent's face, showing disrespect for the referee, etc. A penalty foul includes knocking down the goal cage to prevent an opponent scoring.

Water Polo (Women)
Water polo for women was introduced to the Olympic calendar at Sydney in 2000. The inclusion of this sport proved to be a bonus for Australia which took the gold medal. The United States

Chapter Four: Aquatics to Athletics

received the silver medal and Russia was awarded the bronze.

Winners of MORE THAN ONE GOLD MEDAL in aquatics (swimming, diving, water polo) in one Olympiad, 1988-

SEOUL: 1988
Men
Matt Biondi (USA): 50m freestyle: 100m freestyle: 4 x 100m freestyle: 4 x 200m freestyle: 4 x 100m medley.
Tamas Darnyi (Hungary): 200m medley and 400m medley.
Greg Louganis (USA) Springboard Diving and Highboard Diving.
Women
Kristin Otto (German Democratic Republic): 50m freestyle, 100m freestyle, 100m backstroke, 100m butterfly, 4 x 100m freestyle relay and 4 x100m medley. (*Now found to have used performance enhancing drugs throughout her career.*)
Janet Evans (USA): 400m freestyle, 800m freestyle and 400m medley.

BARCELONA: 1992
Men
Alexander Popov (Unified Team: Commonwealth of Independent States): 50m freestyle and 100m freestyle.
Tamas Darnyi (Hungary) 200m medley and 400m medley.
Yevgeni Sadovi (Unified Team: Commonwealth of Independent States): 200m freestyle and 400m free style.
Women
Krisztina Egerszegi (Hungary) 100m backstroke, 200m backstroke and 400m medley.

ATLANTA: 1996
Men
Alexander Popov (Russia): 50m freestyle and 1,000m freestyle.
Danyon Loader (New Zealand) 200m freestyle and 400m

Chapter Four: Aquatics to Athletics

freestyle.
Denis Pankratov (Russia) 100m butterfly and 200m butterfly.
Women
Penelope Heyns (South Africa) 100m breaststroke and 200m breaststroke.
Michelle Smith (Ireland) 400m freestyle, 200m medley and 400m medley.
Fu Mingxia (China) Springboard Diving and Highboard Diving.

SYDNEY: 2000
Men
Pieter van den Hoogenband (The Netherlands) 100m freestyle and 200m freestyle.
Lenny Krayzelburg (USA) 100m backstroke and 200m backstroke.
Domenico Fioravanti (Italy) 100m breaststroke and 200m breaststroke.
Ni Xiong (China) Springboard Diving and Diving 3m Synchronised Springboard (with H. Xiao).
Women
Inge de Bruijn (Netherlands) 50m freestyle, 100m freestyle and 100m butterfly.
Brooke Bennett (USA) 400m freestyle and 800m freestyle.
Diana Mocanu (Romania) 100m backstroke and 200m backstroke.
Yana Klochkova (Ukraine) 200m medley and 400m medley.

ATHENS: 2004
Men
Ian Thorpe (Australia) 300m freestyle and 400m freestyle.
Aaron Peirsol (USA) 100m backstroke and 200m backstroke.
Kosuke Kitajima (Japan) 100m breaststroke and 200m breaststroke.
Michael Phelps (USA). 100m butterfly, 200m butterfly, 200m

Chapter Four: Aquatics to Athletics

individual relay, 4 x 200m freestyle medley, 400m individual medley and 4 x 100m medley relay.

Women

Yana Klochkova (Ukraine). 200m individual relay, 400m individual relay, Springboard Diving and Synchronised 3m Springboard Diving (with Minxia Wu).

Gold medal winning teams for Water Polo, 1988-

Seoul: 1988	Barcelona: 1992	Atlanta: 1996
Yugoslavia	Italy	Spain
	Men's event	**Women's event**
Sydney: 2000	Hungary	Australia
Athens: 2004	Hungary	Italy
Beijing: 2008	....	....
London: 2012	....	....

China makes its mark in Aquatics!

It was at the 1988 Summer Games that China made a significant stride forward in the swimming events, building on its successes in the 1984 Los Angeles Games at which Chinese swimmers earned one gold medal, one silver medal and one bronze medal. (China's final tally in all events held in Los Angeles in 1984 totalled fifteen gold medals, eight silver medals and nine bronze medals).

    In 1988 Chinese swimmers earned two gold medals and five silver medals (two by men and three by women). The tally increased in 1992 to seven gold medals, two silver medals and one bronze medal. The results in 1996 were not quite as successful, but still substantial, with four gold medals, four silver medals and three bronze medals. In Sydney, in 2000, China earned five gold and five silver medals. In the 2004 Athens Games, China won an overall total of sixty-three medals. In the swimming events, the country won seven gold medals, three

48   Forward to Beijing! A Guide to the Summer Olympics

Chapter Four: Aquatics to Athletics

silver medals and one bronze medal.

Archery

Archeologists have established that bows and arrows were employed by hunters in Africa more than 25,000 years ago. Much later in the history of the world, we have evidence that they were used in Greece when the ancient Olympic Games began. Archers played a significant part in the defeat of the French by the English in the crucial battle of Agincourt fought in the year 1415 and they proved to be the weapons of choice in Europe and elsewhere until they gave way to cannons and gunpowder, a substance invented by the Chinese in the 10th century but not adopted by most countries until 400 years later. After the decline of the bow as a weapon, the sport of archery developed as a pastime.

Archery was first added to the modern Summer Olympic Games in 1900 where French and Belgian archers dominated all six events. The number of separate archery events was reduced in the 1904 Summer Games. These were the first Games in which women were given the opportunity to compete in archery as well as men. In the 1908 London Summer Games, there were only two archery events for men and one event for women. The sport was dropped from the programme in 1912 but returned in 1920 with nine events for men, some on fixed targets and some on moving bird targets. After 1920 archery was omitted from the Olympic Programme until 1972 when the event was reintroduced for both men and women.

Useful Terms: Archery

Bow	Today, a bow is usually made of wood with fiberglass, ceramic, foam or carbon fibre.
Arrow	An arrow has a shaft of carbon or aluminium with a steel head.
Fistmele	The archer uses the breadth of a fist and an

Chapter Four: Aquatics to Athletics

	extended thumb to check the distance between the bow and the strings.
"Fletchings"	These assist the flight of the arrow. They are usually made of birds' feathers.
Nock	A notch at the end of an arrow.
Recurve bow	A bow with a single string, attached between the ends of the bow.
Rover	A target chosen at random.
End	A group of arrows, usually three, shot in one sequence before the archer goes to the target to retrieve them.

The Rules of the Game: Archery

The rules of archery competitions are quite complex and, over the years, have undergone considerable modification.

Beginning in 1996, sixty-four competitors in the individual events have been "seeded" from a qualification round. All sixty-four now advance to an elimination round, with the highest qualifier playing the lowest qualifier, the second highest qualifier playing the next lowest qualifier, and so on. In all matches until the finals, eighteen arrows are shot at 70m. Twelve arrows are shot in the quarter finals, semifinals and final. The final round is narrowed down to eight archers. Each of these eight archers shoots four "ends" of three arrows each, making a total of twelve.

Each national archery team has three archers. Each competing team shoots three "ends" of nine arrows each, with each archer shooting one end.

The target is usually made of paper and it must have a diameter of 122cm. It is divided into five concentric rings of different colours and each ring is divided in half making a total of ten concentric areas. The points values of the rings are as follows:

Gold inner: 10 points; Gold outer: 9 points; Red inner: 8

Chapter Four: Aquatics to Athletics

points; Red outer: seven points; Blue inner: six points; Blue outer: five points; Black inner: four points; Black outer: three points; White inner: two points; White outer: one point. If an arrow touches two rings then the ring with the highest point score is counted. If an arrow misses the target, of course, no points are scored.

Most competitors qualify to take part through their performances at the most recent World Target Championships. Others qualify as the result of their performances in five regional tournaments. Three places are reserved for the host nation and three places are selected by the International Archery Federation.

Gold medal winners in Archery, 1988-
(For individual events; athletes' names are given. For team events, the countries represented are listed.)

	Men	Women
Seoul: 1988	Jay Barrs (USA) Team: South Korea	Kim Soo Nyung (South Korea) Team: South Korea
Barcelona: 1992	Sebastian Flute (France) Team: Spain	Cho Youn-Jeong (South Korea) Team: (South Korea)
Atlanta: 1996	Justin Huish (USA) Team: USA	Kim Kyung-Wook (Korea) Team: South Korea
Sydney: 2000	Simon Fairweather (Australia) Team: Korea.	Mi-Jin Yun (Korea) Team: South Korea
Athens: 2004	Galiazzo Marco	Park Sung Hyun

Chapter Four: Aquatics to Athletics

	(Italy)	(Korea)
	Team: South Korea	Team: South Korea
Beijing: 2004	……………..	………………..
	………………...	…………………..
	…………………	…………………..
London: 2012	……………..	………………..
	………………...	…………………...
	………………...	…………………...

Athletics

More than twice the number of men's athletic events were included in the Summer Games of 2004 in Athens, as compared to those held in the same city in 1896. The 1896 men's athletic events were also distinctive in that four men earned two gold medals each. Thomas Burke was the winner in both the 100m and 400m races. Edwin Flack led the pack in each of the 800m and 1500m races. Ellery Clark was successful in both the High Jump and the Long Jump and Robert Garrett triumphed in both the Shot and the Discus.

Although they had taken part in Olympic swimming events since 1912, women did not participate in Olympic athletics until the Summer Games of 1928 when they competed with each other in the 100m, 800m and 4x100m races, as well as in the High Jump and the Discus.

Field Events

These events are divided into jumping events (long jump, triple jump, high jump and pole vault) and throwing events (shot put, discus, javelin and hammer throw).

Jumping Events: Format and Rules
Long Jump

The long jump area should preferably be 45m long. To be valid, a jump must be made from behind a board that is 20cm wide. Each jump is measured from a dent in the sand made by the jumper's

Chapter Four: Aquatics to Athletics

limbs or body. After selection from a qualifying round, all the finalists are allowed three jumps each. The first eight finalists are then allowed three more jumps.

Triple Jump (the Hop, Step and Jump)
Jumpers should run at full speed before they hop, step and jump. Contestants must land on the same foot that they use when they start their jumps.

A jump is declared a foul in the following circumstances: when a competitor oversteps the take-off board, misses the pit entirely, or does not perform the attempt within an allotted amount of time (usually about one minute).

High Jump
Competitors in this event must take off from one foot and clear a crossbar of 4m in length. The distance to the bar should preferably be 25m long. Competitors may begin at any height they choose. A competitor is eliminated after three unsuccessful attempts, even if the bar is at different heights. It is possible to touch the crossbar, provided that it does not fall. The athlete with the fewest misses at the last cleared height wins the competition.

Pole Vault
Competitors are given two minutes to make a vault, using a pole of any length. The runway must be 45m long. The pole is placed in a sunken box that is one metre long and 60cm wide in the front. The crossbar must be 4.5m long. Vaulters are allowed to touch the crossbar but must not dislodge it.

Throwing Events: Format and Rules
Discus Throw
In this ancient sport, the competitor must throw a discus weighing two kilograms and with a diameter of 22cm.

Hammer Throw
The hammer must be thrown from a circle measuring 2.135m in diameter; the hammer weighs sixteen pounds and it is attached to a grip by a steel wire that should not be longer than 121.5cm.

Chapter Four: Aquatics to Athletics

Javelin Throw
Competitors must release a wooden or metal-shafted javelin from the shoulder whilst running. The javelin should weigh 800grams and measure between 2.60m and 2.70m.

Decathlon
In this event, athletes must take part in ten events over a period of two days. These are the 100m dash, the 400m run, the 110m hurdles, the 1,500m run, the long jump, the high jump, the shot put, the discus throw, the pole vault and the javelin throw. The rules differ little from those applying to each separate event. In the running events, however, the competitors are allowed two false starts and in the throwing events and the long jump, each athlete is allowed only three attempts. The competitors score points based on tables accepted by the International Amateur Athletics Federation. Electronic means are used in timing. In the event of two competitors finishing all ten events with the same total of points, the winner is declared to be the competitor with the highest total in the most separate events.

Useful Terms: High Jump

Brill bend	The same as the Fosbury Flop (named after the American athlete, Dick Fosbury). The head and shoulders are thrown over the bar first and the legs are pulled back to ensure a good clearance.
Increment	The distance that a bar is moved upwards after each successful jump.
Scissors	Clearing the bar with the legs only and without rotating the hips. A training technique.
Starting height	The height of the bar that is determined before the final of the long jump competition begins.
Straddle	The jumper keeps his or her legs wide apart and the body straight.

Chapter Four: Aquatics to Athletics

| Western roll | The athlete throws his or her front leg over the bar. The body and the other leg roll over, parallel to the bar. |

Track Events

The Rules of the Game

Men
Running
100m
Each runner is allowed one false start only in this race in which each lane is between 1.22m and 1.25m wide.
200m
There is a staggered start to this race but all runners run the same distance.
400m
This one-lap race is also run with a staggered start.
800m
This is a two-lap race with a staggered start. The runners must stay in their lanes until the end of the first curve in the track. Then they can run to the inside.
1,500m
Twelve runners take part in the final of this race that is run over three and three-quarter laps.
5,000m
Fifteen runners take part in the final of this race that is run over 12 and a half laps. It requires the competitors to employ a variety of tactics. For example, is it wise to take the lead and try to remain in that position throughout the race? Sometimes this tactic works but often it does not.
10,000m
Twenty runners participate in the final of this race that is run over 25 laps.

Chapter Four: Aquatics to Athletics

3,000m Steeplechase
In this testing race, competitors must clear seven water jumps and 28 hurdles. The tops of the hurdles are wide enough to allow competitors to step on them. Twelve runners take part in the final of the race.

Hurdles
110m hurdles:
Ten hurdles, each of 1.07m in height, must be cleared by the competitors. A distance of 13.7m is covered to the first hurdle. The distance between the hurdles is 9.1m.
400m hurdles:
In this event, the competitors must jump ten three-foot hurdles. The distance from the start to the first hurdle must be 45m and the distance between the hurdles must be 35m.

Relays
4x100m relay
This is a one-lap race with a staggered start. The baton, weighing at least 50grams, must be 28 to 30cm long and between 12cm and 13cm in circumference, If a runner drops the baton, he may leave his lane to recover it, providing that this does not reduce the total distance to be covered. The competitors must exchange batons in a 20m passing area. If the baton is passed outside a zone, then the runner is disqualified.
4x400m relay
This is another race that begins with a staggered start. The first runner stays in his or her lane. The second runner may move to the inside after the first bend. The third and fourth runners station themselves from one lane out, depending upon the order of their teammates when they are half a lap distant. Runners must stay in their lanes after transferring the baton, so as not to obstruct other teams.

Chapter Four: Aquatics to Athletics

Walking
20,000m Walk
Walking races are held on a road. The rules state that the competitors must always keep at least one foot in contact with the ground. Walkers must also straighten their legs at each step when they first contact the ground.

50,000m Walk
The rules for this exhausting race are the same as those applying to for the 20,000m walk.

The Marathon
A reminder of the ancient Games, the marathon must take place on roads. This is a regulation similar to that applying to the 20,000m and 5,000m walks. The marathon must, however, finish within a stadium.

Women
Running
100m
An automatic timing system must be used in events shorter than the 400m dash. The competitors gain power and traction by placing their feet in metal starting blocks behind the starting line. Competitors must pay close attention to the starting pistol so that false starts can be avoided. In such a short race, the sprinters who are fastest out of the starting blocks have an immediate advantage.

200m
This race is started at the curve of the track. The athletes are not permitted to run inside the inner curve, nor are they allowed to step on the inner line of the track. All competitors in the finals must have participated in the heats. Athletes who finish in the top positions in the heats qualify for the next phase of the competition.

Chapter Four: Aquatics to Athletics

400m
Sometimes known as the "endurance sprint", this is the longest "sprinting" competition at the Olympics. At the beginning of the race, the athletes are spread out so that each covers the same distance. After a first false start, an athlete is given a warning by the judge. Two false starts lead to disqualification. The athletes are not allowed to step on the inner line of the track and are also prohibited from running inside the inner curve of the track. Athletes who deliberately obstruct other competitors are liable to be disqualified.
800m
Runners are allowed to break away from their original lanes after the first bend in the track has been reached.
1,500m
Strategy plays an important role in this race. Contestants will not try to break away too soon or too late. Runners are allowed to break lanes almost immediately after the start of the race.
5,000m
Runners are allowed to break lanes immediately after the start of the race.
10,000m
This is the longest track event in the Olympics. Like men, women runners usually prepare themselves by competing in cross country events and road races.

Hurdles
100m hurdles (women)
The women's 100m hurdles race differs from the men's in that women are expected to clear hurdles that are only 0.838 metres high. The distance from the starting point to the first hurdle is 13m and there are eight and a half metres between hurdles. The distance from the last hurdle to the finish is ten and a half metres.
400m hurdles (women)
The hurdles are 0.762m high.

Chapter Four: Aquatics to Athletics

Shot Put, Discus and Javelin (women)
The women's shot weights four kilograms. The discus weighs one kilogram and the javelin weighs six hundred grams.

Heptathlon (men and women)
The athletes compete in seven events: the 100m hurdles, the high jump, the short put, the 200m dash, the long jump, the javelin and the 800m run. As in the men's pentathlon, points are scored based on tables accepted by the International Amateur Athletics Federation.

Winners of MORE THAN ONE gold medal in Athletics in a single Olympiad, 1988-2004 (individual & team events combined)

1988: SEOUL
Men
Carl Lewis (USA)   100m, Long Jump, 4x 400m relay

Women
Florence Griffith-Joyner (USA) 100m, 200m, 4x100m relay
Jackie Joyner-Kersee (USA)   Long jump, heptathlon

1992: BARCELONA
Men
Carl Lewis (USA)   Long Jump and 4x100m

1996: ATLANTA
Men
Michael Johnson (USA)   200m and 400m
Carl Lewis (USA)   Long Jump, 4x100m and 4x400m relay

Chapter Four: Aquatics to Athletics

Women
Marie-José Perec (France)	200m and 400m
Svetlana Masterkova (Russia)	800m and 1,500m
USA	4x100m and 4x400m relay

SYDNEY 2000
Men
Robert Korzeniowski (Poland)	20km walk and 50km walk
USA	4x100m relay and 4x400m relay

Women
Marion Jones (USA)	100m, 200m and 4 x 400m relay.

Note: In 2007, Marion Jones was found guilty of using performance-enhancing drugs and was stripped of the medals that she won in Sydney.

ATHENS: 2004
Men
Jeremy Wariner (USA)	400m and 4 x 400m relay
El Guerrouj Hicham (Morocco)	1,500m and 5,000m

Women
Kelly Holmes (Great Britain)	800m and 1,500m
Veronica Campbell (USA)	200m and 4x100m relay

Some Key Words

Aquatic	Coefficient	Marathon
Artistry	Discus	Rigid
Archaeological	Exclusion	Shot Put
Backstroke	Heptathlon	Turbulence
Breaststroke	Inclusion	Vaulter
Butterfly	Javelin	Zone

Chapter Four: Aquatics to Athletics

QUIZ
1. How long must an Olympic swimming pool be?
2. What is the nickname of the Beijing National Swimming Centre?
3. Why have a number of athletes taken legal action against the German government?
4. How many different strokes are there in Olympic swimming? What are they?
5. How many players must there be on a Water Polo team?
6. How many gold medals did China win in the 2004 Olympic swimming competition?
7. In what year did archery become an Olympic sport?
8. Why were the men's athletic events distinctive in the 1896 Olympic Games?
9. How many attempts may an athlete make in the Olympic high jump event before being disqualified?
10. How many sports are there in the decathlon event?
11. How many sports are there in the heptathlon event?
12. Which events do the following pictograms represent?

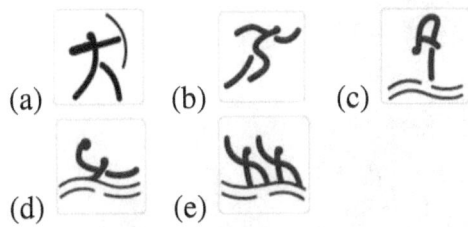

Forward to Beijing! A Guide to the Summer Olympics

LO Ting Wai (L) & SO Sau Wah (R). Canoeing, Asian Games, 1-15 December 2007, held in Doha, the capital of Qatar, United Arab Emirates. *Photo Courtesy SFOCHKC.*

WONG Kam Po (L1), Doha Asian Games, 2007. *Photo Courtesy SFOCHKC.* ~ Important in themselves, these Games were a good preparation and selection tool for the Beijing Summer Olympics, 2008.

Chapter Five: Badminton to Cycling

Chapter Five

BADMINTON TO CYCLING

Badminton is a relatively modern version of the ancient game of battledore and shuttlecock played in ancient times in Greece, China and India. In more recent times, the game was taken up by British army officers in India who drew up the first rules for a game they then called "poona".

The word "shuttlecock" refers to the flighted "bird" that is made of a combination of bird feathers, leather, cork, string and glue. The name badminton derives its name from Badminton House in England.

Badminton was introduced as a demonstration sport at the 1972 Olympics. It was added to the Olympic programme at the 1992 Barcelona Summer Games. Originally, a gentle game, it is today fast and sometimes furious. Leather-covered shuttles topped by goose feathers are driven over the net at speeds that can top 150 miles per hour.

Useful Terms: Badminton

Back Alley	The area at the back of the Badminton Court.
Drive	A fast and low shot that causes the shuttle to fly over the net horizontally.
Lob	A shot that causes the shuttle to fly high into the air.
Smash	A hard hit overhead shot that propels the shuttle straight down into the opponent's court.
A Drop Shot	A soft but skillful shot that causes the shuttle to fall rapidly and close to the net in the opponents' court.

Chapter Five: Badminton to Cycling

The Rules of the Game: Badminton

There are precise requirements for the layout of a badminton court. This must be 13.4m long and the net must be 1.55m high. The playing area must be 5.18m wide for singles games and 6.1m wide for doubles. To win, 15 points must be earned in the men's singles and women's doubles game and 11 points must be earned in the women's singles' game. Only the server may score points. Badminton is now a direct elimination competition. The eight highest ranking players or teams are seeded and the remaining players are chosen by a blind draw.

Note: Badminton was included in the Olympic Games for the first time in 1992.

Gold medal winners in Badminton, 1992-

BARCELONA: 1992
Men
Alan Budi Kusuma (Indonesia)	Singles
South Korea (Kim Moon-Soo/Park Joo-Bong)	Doubles

Women
Susi Susanti (Indonesia),	Singles
South Korea (Hwang Hye-Young/Chung So-Young)	Doubles

ATLANTA 1996
Men
Poul-Erik Hoyer-Larsen (Denmark)	Singles
Rexy Mainmaky/Ricky Subagia (Indonesia)	Doubles

Chapter Five: Badminton to Cycling

Women
Bang Soo-Hyun (Korea)	Singles
Ge Fei/Gu Jun) (China)	Doubles
Kim Dong-Moon/Gill Young-Ah (South Korea)	Mixed Doubles

SYDNEY 2000
Men
Ji Xinpeng (China)	Singles
Tony Gunawan/Candra Wijaya (Indonesia)	Doubles

Women
Gong Zhichao (China)	Singles
Ge Fei/Gu Jun (China)	Doubles
Zhang Jun/Gao Ling (China)	Mixed Doubles

ATHENS 2004
Men
Taufik Hidayat (Indonesia)	Singles
South Korea (Kim Dong Moon/Ha Tae Kwon)	Doubles

Women
Zhang Ning (China)	Singles
Zhang Jiewen/Yang Wei (China)	Doubles
China Zhang Jun/Gao Ling (China)	Mixed Doubles

Baseball
Baseball was added to the Olympic programme in 1992. Although it receives considerable support from the U.S. media at home and abroad, baseball is not exclusively an American game. This seems to have been proved in 1992, when Cuba was awarded the gold medal, and by Cuba's subsequent successes.

Chapter Five: Badminton to Cycling

Lovers of cricket sometimes wonder why baseball was introduced for the first time in the Olympic programme in 1992, while cricket has only appeared once, in 1900. But then there are also those who feel that other games should have been retained. For example, croquet (1900 only), golf (1900 and 1904 only), lacrosse (1904 and 1908 only), motor boating (1908 only) and polo (1900, 1908 and 1920 only).

Useful Terms: Baseball

Balk	An illegal action when a pitcher pretends a throw to base or a pitch.
Battery	The pitcher and the catcher (originally the pitcher only)
Beanball	A pitch aimed at the batter's head, causing him to duck under the ball.
Bunt	The batter lets the ball hit the bat but does not swing at it. This may force a fielder away from the base and give the batter a chance to run safely to first base or give a third-base runner the chance to reach home base.
Curveball	The pitcher spins the ball so that it curves to the left.
Double play	This involves the first and second basemen and short stop. Its purpose is to put out two opponents in a single action.
Fastball	The pitcher throws the ball at high speed and with backward spin.
Home run	A hit that allows a batter to make a complete circuit of the bases. There is a home base and first, second and third bases.
Homer	A home run.
Jamming	The pitcher aims the ball at the batter's body, affecting his swing.

Chapter Five: Badminton to Cycling

Knuckleball	A flat row with no spin on the ball.
Out	One of the three required retirements of an offensive team during its time at bat.
Put out	An attempt to put out a base runner when the ball is hit.
Screwball	The pitcher throws the ball like a curveball but the spin is reversed so that the ball breaks downwards and to the right.
Short stop	The fielding position of the player on a baseball team who is stationed between second and third base.
Slider	The ball is pitched so that it breaks less than a curveball and closer to the batter.
Strike	The batter misses the ball.
Sweet spot	The batter can achieve maximum power by using this particular part of the bat.
Squeeze play	A method used by the batting team to help the man at third base to get safely home.
Steal bases	The player tries to reach a base without the striker hitting the ball.
Tagged out	The runner fails to touch base before being tagged.
Tagg	The action of a fielder in touching a base with his body while holding the ball in his hand or glove, or touching a runner with the ball while holding the ball in his hand or glove.

The Rules of the Game: Baseball

The rules for baseball may be complicated for the newcomer to the game to understand, although some say that these rules are not as complicated as cricket. The "pitch" or field in baseball has an infield and an outfield. The infield is laid out with four bases, or

Chapter Five: Badminton to Cycling

"diamonds" that must be 27.4m apart including the "home plate". The distance between the "home plate" and the "pitcher's mound" is 18.43m. The pitcher's mound is a raised area from which the pitcher throws the ball at the batter.

Each of two teams has nine players who may be substituted at any time. Runs are scored when the batter runs from home plate to first base and then to the second and third bases, before returning to the home plate. Players are "out" if a member of the opposing team catches the ball before it touches the ground (as in cricket), or if an opposition player touches first base with the ball in his hand before the batter reaches the base. The batter may also be declared out at the second or third bases if he is unable to reach them before the fielder has possession of the ball. A batter may also be "out" if he or she "strikes out" (i.e. fails to hit the ball after it has been pitched at him three times). When three outs have occurred, the teams change sides. An "inning" is declared when both teams have had the opportunity to bat. A full game lasts for nine innings.

Olympic baseball is played by eight teams. After preliminary games, the top four teams advance to the semi-finals. The team in first place plays the fourth-place team and the second-placed team competes against the third placed.

Gold medal winning teams in Baseball, 1992-

Barcelona: 1992 Cuba	Atlanta:1996 Cuba	Sydney: 2000 USA
Athens: 2004 Cuba	Beijing: 2008	London: 2012 ....

Basketball
It is generally agreed that basketball was invented by Dr James Naismith, a Canadian, born in 1861. Naismith attended McGill University as a student and, after graduation, became the University's Athletics Director. After some years in that post, he

Chapter Five: Badminton to Cycling

was employed at the YMCA Training School in Springfield, Massachusetts. It was while he was at the YMCA that Naismith introduced basketball, a game that, although strenuous, could be played indoors and would not be hampered by changes in the weather.

After some years at Springfield, Naismith qualified as a medical doctor specializing in sport psychology. He later became a Presbyterian Minister.

Basketball was included in the Olympic Games programme for the first time in 1936.

Useful Terms: Basketball

Assist	The final pass given to the shooter.
Backcourt	The area from the midcourt line to the end line furthest from the offense's basket.
Basket	A metal rim with a corded net hanging off it; attached to a backboard.
Block	Illegal physical contact that interferes with an opponent who does not have the ball.
Double foul	Two players commit personal or technical fouls at approximately the same time in the same situations.
Dunk	Shooting so that the hands are above the ring and the ball drops down through the hoop.
Eight-second rule	A team should not be possession of the ball in its backcourt for more than eight (consecutive) seconds.
End line	The line behind each basket; also called the baseline.
Field Goal	An attempt to score from the area inside

Chapter Five: Badminton to Cycling

	the three-point field goal line. If successful, this counts for two points. A successful attempt outside the three-point line counts for three points.
Free Throw	An unhindered shot from the free-throw line given to penalise the other team for committing a foul.
Held Ball	Two opponents have one or two hands firmly on the ball and neither can gain possession.
Illegal Assist	It is not permitted for a player to use the basket ring to hold, lift or raise himself. Neither may assist a teammate to gain height while attempting to score.
Jump Ball	The referee tosses the ball between two opponents. Each tries to tap it to a teammate.
Key	The area between the free-throw line and the endline, bordered by two angled lines, in which no offensive player may stand for three seconds at a time.
Live ball	A ball is live as soon as given to a free-throw shooter or a thrower on a throw-in.
Loose Ball Foul	Illegal contact after the ball is live.
Personal Foul	A player holds, impedes or pushes an opponent. Up to three free throws may be awarded against the offending team.
Pick	A play, without causing contact which prevents an opponent from reaching a particular position.
Pivot	The foot must remain touching the floor until a ball handler who has stopped dribbling is ready to pass or shoot.
Press	Harassing opponents into hurried play.

Chapter Five: Badminton to Cycling

Screen	(Same as "pick".)
Shooter	A player who takes a shot at the basket.
Technical Fouls	Misconduct that officials believe is detrimental to the game. This is penalised by a free-throw opportunity to the non-offending team.
Timeouts	A break in play during a game.
Three-Second rule	A player must not stand for more than three seconds in the free throw lane when the ball is in his team's control.
Three-point shot	A field goal worth three points because the shooter was standing behind the three-point line when he released the ball.
Turnover	A team loses possession of the ball before any member has been able to try for a basket.
Travel	To run with the ball without bouncing it.
24-Second Clock	A team must try to score a field goal within twenty-four seconds after obtaining possession of the ball.
Two-minute period	The game is in the two-minute period when only ten minutes of play remain.

The Rules of the Game: Basketball

Basketball is played on a court 28m long and 15m wide. The purpose of the game is to shoot the ball into a basket that is situated 3.05m above the ground at each end of the court. A basket ring should be 45.8cm in diameter and painted orange. If the ball lands in the net, it earns two points for the shooter. If he or she throws the ball successfully from a "three point" line, then three points may be earned. This line is marked out 6.24m from the basket.

Chapter Five: Badminton to Cycling

Each basketball team has five players who play two halves, each lasting for twenty minutes. A player whose team is in possession of the ball must not spend more than three seconds in the opposing team's restricted area. This is an area that extends for 3m on each side of a basket, beginning at an endline. Each team is allowed two "time-outs" (i.e. rests) per half and a time-out may be called by the team's coach. After a shot is made, balls bouncing on the rim of the net may be touched.

Gold medal winning teams in Basketball, 1988-

	Men	**Women**
Seoul: 1988	USSR	USA
Barcelona: 1992	USA	Unified Team
Atlanta: 1996	USA	USA
Sydney: 2000	USA	USA
Athens: 2004	Argentina	USA
Beijing: 2008	………………..	……………….
London: 2012	………………..	……………….

Beach Volleyball

As athletic director of the Beach Club at Santa Monica, California, the Olympic swimming champion, Duke Kahanamoku, played a major role in developing beach volleyball. Following on from the initiatives taken by Kahanamoku, the Santa Monica Recreation Department staged the first of four annual beach volleyball tournaments in 1944. Gradually the game began to be recognized as a serious sport and the California Beach Volleyball Association was established in 1965 to standardize rules. By the nineteen eighties, the sport had spread to other countries. In 1986 an international competition was held in Brazil and a professional association was established in Australia in 1987. In 1996, Beach Volleyball was added to the Olympic programme in Atlanta and the sport was included in the two Olympic competitions held since then, in Sydney and in Athens.

Chapter Five: Badminton to Cycling

Useful Terms: Beach Volleyball

Block	A basic return at the net to block a "spike".
Duration	All Olympic beach volleyball matches are best two-out-of-three sets. The first two sets are played to twenty-one points. The third set, if necessary, is played to fifteen points. In each set, a team must win by at least a two-point margin; there is no ceiling, so play continues until one team goes ahead by two points, thus winning the game.
Side change	Teams change sides of the court at every multiple of five points until the match has finished. This is intended to equalize the effect of the sun and wind on the outcome of the game.
Spike	An attacking shot made with one hand from across and above the net.
Volley	A two-handed shot over the net or for another team member to spike.
Time-outs	Each team is allowed to call one, 30-second, time-out in each set. Players may request a time-out when the ball is out of play and before the whistle is blown to signal a serve.

The Rules of the Game: Beach Volleyball

As mentioned above, Beach Volleyball was introduced for the first time at the Atlanta Games. It differs from its sister, Volleyball, in three ways: there are only two players on each team; the court is made of sand (unlike Volleyball) and only the serving team can score a point. All matches are best-of-three sets, the first two being played to twenty-one and the third to fifteen. It is necessary for a team to gain at least two points to win a set.

Chapter Five: Badminton to Cycling

Beach Volleyball at the Olympics
The competition at the Beijing Olympics will have two stages: qualification and single elimination:

For qualification, twenty-four teams will be divided into six pools of four teams. The teams will follow a "round robin" format, playing each of the three teams in their pool once. The rankings in each pool will be based on the ratio of matches won or lost, the ratio of sets won or lost and the ratio of points won or lost during pool play. If two teams remain tied after the previous criteria have been applied, a coin toss will be used to determine the higher ranking.

Single elimination: The top two teams in each pool (a total of twelve), together with the four best third-ranked teams, advance to a sixteen-team, single elimination round. At this stage, the winner of a match progresses and the loser is eliminated. The tournament will continue in single elimination format until the semi-finals, after which the two winning teams will compete for the gold medal and the two losing teams will play in a bronze-medal match.

Gold medal winning teams in Beach volleyball, 1988-

	Men's Pairs	**Women's Pairs**
Atlanta: 1996	USA	Brazil
Sydney: 2000	USA	Australia
Athens: 2004	Brazil	USA
Beijing: 2008	…………..	…………….
London: 2012	…………..	…………….

Boxing
Usually listed as a "combative sport", boxing was introduced to the Olympics in 1904 but was in and out of the Games until added (for good?) in 1920. Olympic boxing has proved to be an excellent training ground for fighters who later found success as

Chapter Five: Badminton to Cycling

professionals. Among the well-known boxers who began their careers at the Olympic level were Cassius Clay (Muhammad Ali), Joe Frazier, George Forman, Floyd Patterson and Lennox Lewis.

Until 2000, Olympic boxing consisted of three three-minute rounds with one-minute breaks between rounds. In the year 2000, this arrangement was modified and the boxers now fight four two-minute rounds with a one minute break in between each round.

Useful Terms: Boxing

Belt	An imaginary line from the navel to the top of the hips. Opposing boxers are not allowed to hit below the belt.
Bout	A boxing contest; also called a match.
Caution	An advance warning.
Concede	The end of a fight when one of the boxers' admits that he cannot win.
Head-butts	Strikes that use the top of one's head to attack others.
Southpaw	A boxer who leads with the right hand.
Switch-hitting	To change from orthodox (leading with the left hand) to southpaw during a match.
Throwing in the towel	The traditional declaration of defeat in boxing when as assistant (a "Second") who considers that his boxer cannot continue the bout throws a towel into the ring. This is a sign that the boxer has conceded the fight.

Chapter Five: Badminton to Cycling

The Rules of the Game: Boxing

In Olympic boxing, there are 12 categories, ranging from light-flyweight (115 1/4 pounds minus) to super-heavyweight (200 1/2 pounds plus). During a fight, a referee is inside the ring with the competitors. There are four judges at the ringside to keep scores.

Some precautions are now taken to protect fighters from serious injury. A boxer is required to wear protective headgear and a vest. The referee can stop the bout when one of the boxers has been knocked to the floor of the ring and is unable to stand up after a count of ten seconds. When the boxer is able to get up within the ten seconds, he is forbidden to resume fighting until a count of eight has been given. If a boxer is knocked down three times in one round, or four times in a fight, he is regarded as having lost the bout. When a boxer's assistant ("second") considers that his man can no longer fight, he can concede the bout by throwing a towel into the ring.

Some blows are forbidden. Boxers are not allowed to throw an open-handed punch or a forearm punch. Punching behind the head, below the belt or at the kidneys is not allowed and head butts are also banned. A caution is given when one of these fouls is committed; two cautions constitute a warning and three cautions result in disqualification.

The boxers are drawn together in random pairs and fight in a knockout tournament. The two semi-final winners compete for the gold and silver medals while both losers receive bronze.

Gold medal winners in Boxing, 1988-

SEOUL: 1988
Ivailo Christov (Bulgaria)	Light Flyweight
Kim Kwang Sun (Korea)	Flyweight
Kennedy McKinney (USA)	Bantamweight
Giovanni Parisi (Italy)	Featherweight
Andreas Zulow (German	Lightweight

Chapter Five: Badminton to Cycling

Democratic Republic)	
Vyacheslav Yanovski (Soviet Union)	Light Welterweight
Robert Wangila (Kenya)	Welterweight
Park Si Hun (Korea)	Light Middleweight
Henry Maske (German Democratic Republic)	Middleweight
Andrew Maynard (USA)	Light Heavyweight
Ray Mercer (USA)	Heavyweight
Lennox Lewis (Canada)	Super Heavyweight

BARCELONA: 1992

Rogelio Marcelo Garcia (Cuba)	Light Flyweight
Choi Su Choi (North Korea)	Flyweight
Joel Casamayor (Cuba)	Bantamweight
Andreas Tews (Germany)	Featherweight
Oscar de la Hoya (USA)	Lightweight
Hector Vinent (Cuba)	Light Welterweight
Michael Carruth (Ireland)	Welterweight
Juan Lemus Garcia (Cuba)	Light Middleweight
Ariel Hernandez (Cuba)	Middleweight
Torsten May (Germany)	Light Heavyweight
Felix Savon (Cuba)	Heavyweight
Roberto Balado Mendez (Cuba)	Super Heavyweight

Cuba did extraordinarily well, winning seven gold medals for boxing in these Games.

ATLANTA: 1996

Daniel Petrov (Bulgaria)	Light Flyweight
Maikro Romero (Cuba)	Flyweight
Istvan Kovacs (Hungary)	Bantamweight
Somluk Kamsing (Thailand)	Featherweight
Hocine Soltani (Algeria)	Lightweight
Hector Vinent (Cuba)	Light Welterweight

Chapter Five: Badminton to Cycling

Oleg Saitov (Russia)	Welterweight
David Reid (USA)	Light Middleweight
Ariel Hernandez (Cuba)	Middleweight
Vasili Jirov (Kazakhstan)	Light Heavyweight
Felix Savon (Cuba)	Heavyweight
Vladimir Klichko (Ukraine)	Super Heavyweight

SYDNEY: 2000

Brahim Asloum (France)	Light Flyweight
Wijan Ponlid (Thailand)	Flyweight
Guillermo Rigondeaux (Cuba)	Bantamweight
Bekzat Sattarkhanov (Kazakhstan)	Featherweight
Mario Kindelan (Cuba)	Lightweight
Mahammadkodir Abdullayev (Uzbekistan)	Light Welterweight
Oleg Saitov (Russia)	Welterweight
Yermakhan Ibraimov (Kazakhstan)	Light Middleweight
Jorge Gutierrez (Cuba)	Middleweight
Alexandre Lebziak (Russia)	Light Heavyweight
Felix Savon (Cuba)	Heavyweight
Audley Harrison (Great Britain)	Super Heavyweight

2004: ATHENS

Bhartelemy Varela Yan (Cuba)	Light Flyweight
Gamboa Toledano Yunorkis (Cuba)	Flyweight
Rigondeaux Ortiz Guillermo (Cuba)	Bantamweight
Tichtchenko, Alexei (Russia)	Featherweight
Kindelan Mesa Mario Cesar (Cuba)	Lightweight
Boonjumnong Manus (Thailand)	Light Welterweight
Artayev Bakhtiyar (Khazakstan)	Welterweight
Gaydarbekov Gaydarbek (Russia)	Middleweight
Ward Andre (USA)	Light Heavyweight
Solis Fonte Odlanier (Cuba)	Heavyweight
Povetskin Alexander (Russia)	Super Heavyweight

Chapter Five: Badminton to Cycling

Canoeing

The history of the canoe and kayak can be traced back thousands of years to when people used these craft to travel, fish and hunt. The word "canoe" comes from a Haitian word, "canoa", meaning "a light type of boat propelled by paddles". Skin canoes, probably first used by Canadian Inuits (Eskimos) are known as kayaks. For centuries, canoes were also a means of transport for South American Indians and Pacific Islanders.

In 1975, a replica of a thousand-year old canoe was built in Hawaii and sailed to Tahiti without engines or sails. The navigator (from the island of Palau) steered the vessel by reading the stars and the tides. The full story of this epic voyage has been told in the book, The Hokule'a: The Way to Tahiti by Ben. R. Finney. The canoe is still afloat and is used for educational purposes.

In 1924, canoeing was included in the Paris Olympics as a demonstration sport. It was rejected in 1932 and 1936 but became a full Olympic medal sport at the 1936 Berlin Games.

Useful Terms: Canoeing

Eskimo Roll	A roll over 360 degrees that starts and finishes above water.
Flatwater	Calm water or a slow-moving river current with no rapids.
Quads	A competition of kayak events manned by four paddlers.
Repêchage	A second-chance round (from the French word "repasser", meaning "to go again").
Slalom	A race down a winding course with obstacles.
Whitewater	Turbulent, foaming water.

Chapter Five: Badminton to Cycling

The Rules of the Game: Canoeing

Canoes and kayaks for one person are usually 5.18m long. Boats for two persons are about 6.4m long and kayaks manned by four competitors are usually 11m long. The lanes for racing are usually 9m wide. The canoes and kayaks are required to remain in the middle of their lanes and must not approach within 5m of another boat. Only one false start is acceptable. The winners of each preliminary round qualify to advance to the semi-finals; the remaining competitors participate in a second-chance round known as a "repêchage". The fastest competitors in each repêchage are allowed to participate in the semi-finals. Nine boats can participate in the finals.

Gold medal winners in Canoeing, 1988-
Winning athletes' names and countries are given for individual events. The countries they represented are listed for doubles and fours events.
Key: C: Canoe; K: Kayak; 1: Single; 2: Double/ Pair; 4: Four

SEOUL: 1988
Men

Ivans Klementyev (USSR)	C-1	1000m
Olaf Heukrodt (German Democratic Republic (East Germany))	C-1	500m
The USSR	C-2	1,000m
The USSR	C-2	500m
Gregory Mark Barton (USA)	K-1	1,000m
Zsolt Gyulay (Hungary)	K-1	500m
USA	K-2	1,000m
New Zealand	K-2	500m
Hungary	K-4	1,000m

Women

Vania Guecheva (Bulgaria)	K-1	500m

Chapter Five: Badminton to Cycling

German Democratic Republic (East Germany)	K-2	500m
German Democratic Republic (East Germany)	K-4	500m

BARCELONA: 1992
Men

Nikolai Petkov Bukhalov (Bulgaria)	C-1	1,000m
Nikolai Petkov Bukhalov (Bulgaria)	C-1	500m
Germany	C-2	1,000m
United Team (Commonwealth of Independent States)	C-2	500m
Clint Robinson (Australia)	K-1	1,000m
Mikko Yrjö Kolehmainen (Finland)	K-1	500m
Germany	K-2	1,000m
Germany	K-2	500m
Germany	K-4	1,000m
Lukas Pollert (Czechoslovakia)	C-1	Slalom
USA	C-2	Slalom
Pierpaolo Ferrazzi	K-1	Slalom

Women

Birgit Schmidt (OR Fischer) (Germany)	K-1	500m
Germany	K-2	500m
Hungary	K-4	500m
Elisabeth Micheler-Jones (Germany)	K-1	Slalom

ATLANTA: 1996
Men

Martin Doktor (Czech Republic)	C-1	1,000m
Martin Doktor (Czech Republic)	C-1	500m
Germany	C-2	1,000m
Hungary	C-2	500m
Knut Holmann (Norway)	K-1	1,000m
Antonio Rossi (Italy)	K-1	500m
Italy	K-2	1,000m
Germany	K-2	500m

Chapter Five: Badminton to Cycling

Germany	K-4	1,000m
Michal Martikan (Slovakia)	C-1	Slalom
France	C-2	Slalom
Oliver Fix (Germany)	K-1	Slalom
Women		
Rita Koban (Hungary)	K-1	500m
Sweden	K-2	500m
Germany	K-4	500m
Stepanka Hilgertova (Czech Republic)	K-1	Slalom

SYDNEY: 2000
Men

Andreas Dittmer (Germany)	C-1	1,000m
Gyorgy Kolonics (Hungary)	C-1	500m
Roumania	C-2	1,000m
Hungary	C-2	500m
Knut Holmann (Norway)	K-1	1,000m
Knut Holmann (Norway)	K-1	500m
Italy	K-2	1,000m
Hungary	K-2	500m
Hungary	K-4	1,000m
Tony Estanguet (France)	C-1	Slalom
Slovakia	C-2	Slalom
Thomas Schmidt (Germany)	K-1	Slalom
Women		
Josefa Idem (Italy)	K-1	500m
Germany	K2	500m
Germany	K4	500m
Stepanka Hilgertova (Czech Republic)	K-1	Slalom

ATHENS: 2004
Men

David Cal (Spain)	C-1	1,000m
Andreas Dittmer (Germany)	C-1	500m

Chapter Five: Badminton to Cycling

Germany	C-2	1,000m
China	C-2	500m
Eirik Veraas Larsen (Norway)	K-1	1,000m
Adam Van Koeverden (Canada)	K-1	500m
Sweden	K-2	1,000m
Germany	K-2	500m
Hungary	K-4	1,000m
Tony Estanguet	C-1	Slalom
Slovakia	C-2	Slalom
Benoit Peschier (France)	K-1	Slalom
Women		
Natasa Janics (Hungary)	K-1	500m
Hungary	K-2	500m
Germany	K-4	500m
Elena Kaliska (Slovakia)	K-1	Slalom

Cycling

When the first Olympic cycling event was held in 1896, the Ariel Ordinary bicycle ("penny farthing"), with one large wheel and one small wheel, had been supplanted by a "safety" bicycle, with smaller wheels and a toothed gearwheel connected by a chain with the hub of the rear wheel. This was fortunate for the competitors!

Many changes have taken place since those early days, not only in the technology of bicycle manufacture, but also in the cycling events themselves. For the 2008 Games they have been classified into four disciplines: road races, mountain biking, track races and BMX races.

Useful Terms: Cycling

Attack	A sudden acceleration to move ahead of another rider or riders.
Blind	A sudden spurt.
Bonk	Tiredness, perhaps caused by a lack of food

Chapter Five: Badminton to Cycling

Breakaway	during a race. One or more riders who sprint away from the peloton in an effort to increase their lead.
Broom wagon	The vehicle that follows the race picking up riders who have had to abandon the race.
Keirin	A race in which riders compete in a sprint after completing laps paced by a motorcycle.
Madison	An Olympic cycling contest between two-person teams who alternately ride slowly and quickly.
Parcour	(*French*) The race course.
Peloton	The main group of racers manœuvering for position. Also called "the park".
Points race	A race in which riders are awarded points according to their finishing position in intermediate sprints.
Rail it	To ride fast and clearly through a corner.
Rainbow Jersey	The rainbow-striped jersey awarded to world champions in each of cycling's disciplines.
Ramp	A sloping surface between two places of different levels.
Rotating	The action of each rider going to the front of a group and riding at the front to keep the pace high.
Soigneur	(*French*) An assistant in a cycling team who cares for the riders, including physiotherapy, food preparation, transport, etc.
Velodrome	A banked bicycle racing track.

The Rules of the Game: Cycling

Today, the Olympic programme includes, for both men and women, Road Races (Road Races and Time Trials), Track Races, Mountain Biking and BMX Races.

Chapter Five: Badminton to Cycling

Road Races
"Traditional" road races were included in the Olympic programme from 1896. Men race over 239km and women compete over 120km. The race begins with a mass start and then follows a test of stamina and endurance. Riders who are lapped are required to leave the course unless they are on the final lap. They can legally travel in each other's slipstream, thus allowing them to conserve energy.

Time Trial Races
Time trial races are races against the clock. Men compete over 46.8km whilst women have to cycle 31.2km. The competitors start at ninety-second intervals and are timed over the course. The rider clocking the best time wins the race.

Mountain Bike Cross-Country
Mountain Biking first appeared as an Olympic Sport in 1996 at Atlanta. Riders must be prepared to cycle over fields, forest roads and gravel paths. Tarred and paved roads must not exceed fifteen percent of the total route. Men must race 40km to 50km and women 30km to 40km.

Track Races
Track races take place in a building called a "velodrome". These races include the following individual and team events:
- 1,000m Match Sprint
- 1,000m Time Trial
- 4,000m Individual Pursuit
- 4,000m Team Pursuit
- Olympic Sprint
- Points Race

"Madison" and "Keirin" races were added to the Olympic Games in 2000.

Chapter Five: Badminton to Cycling

"Madison"
This is a contest between two-man teams who alternately ride and sprint every 5km. As the name implies, the "Madison" is named after Madison Square Garden, New York.

"Keirin"
This is a race in which the riders are paced by a motorcycle. At first the motorcycle is driven at 25km per hour. This speed is gradually increased to 45km an hour before the motorcycle leaves the track with two and a half laps still to go. The engine-less cyclists then sprint the remaining distance.

BMX Races
These races will be introduced to the Olympic programme at Beijing in 2008. "BMX" is an abbreviation for "bicycle motor cross", a form of cycling on specially designed bicycles that generally have 51cm wheels.

Winners of gold medals in cycling, 1988-
Winning athletes' names and countries are given for individual events. The countries they represented are listed for team events.

SEOUL 1988
Men

Olaf Ludwig (GDR)	Road Race
GDR	100km. Road Team Time Trial
Lutz Hesslich (GDR)	Sprint
Alexander Kirichenko (Soviet Union)	1,000m. Time Trial
Gintautas Umaras (Soviet Union)	4,000m Individual Pursuit
USSR	4,000m. Team Pursuit
Dan Frost (Denmark)	Individual Points Race

Chapter Five: Badminton to Cycling

Women
Erika Salumae (Soviet Union)   Sprint
Monique Knol (Netherlands)   Road Race

BARCELONA: 1992
Men
Fabio Casartelli (Italy)	Road Race
Germany	100km Road Team Time Trial
Jens Fielder (Germany)	Sprint
Jose Moreno Perinan (Spain)	1,000m. Time Trial
Christopher Boardman (Great Britain)	4,000m. Individual Pursuit
Germany	4,000m. Team Pursuit
Giovanni Lombardi (Italy)	Individual Points Race

Women
Kathryn Watt (Australia)	Road Race
Erika Salumae (Estonia)	Sprint
Petra Rossner (Germany)	3,000m. Individual Pursuit

ATLANTA: 1996
Men
Pascal Richard (Switzerland)	Road Race
Miguel Indurain (Spain)	Road Time Trial
Jens Fielder (Germany)	Sprint
Florian Rousseau (France)	1,000m. Time Trial
Andrea Collinelli (Italy)	4,000m. Individual Pursuit
France	4,000m. Team Pursuit
Silvio Martinello (Italy)	Individual Points Race
Bart Brentjens (Netherlands)	Cross-Country

Women
Jeannie Longo-Ciprelli (France)	Road Race
Zulfia Zabirova (Russia)	Time Trial

Chapter Five: Badminton to Cycling

Felicia Ballanger (France)	Sprint
Antonella Bellutti (Italy)	3,000m. Individual Pursuit
Nathalie Lancien (France)	Individual Points Race
Paola Pezzo (Italy)	Cross-Country

SYDNEY: 2000
Men

Jan Ulrich (Germany)	Road Race
Vyatcheslav Ekimov (Russia)	Road Time Trial
Marty Nothstein (USA)	1,000m. Sprint
France	Olympic Sprint
Jason Queally (Great Britain)	1,000m. Time Trial
Robert Bartko (Germany)	4,000m. Individual Pursuit
Germany	4,000m. Team Pursuit
Juan Llaneras (Spain)	Individual Points Race
Florian Rousseau (France)	Keirin
Australia	Madison
Miguel Martinez (France)	Mountain Bike

Women

Leontien Zijlaard (Netherlands)	Road Race
Leontien Zijlaard (Netherlands)	Time Trial
Felicia Ballanger (France)	500m. Time Trial
Felicia Ballanger (France)	Sprint
Leontien Zijlaard (Netherlands)	3,000m. Individual Pursuit
Antonella Bellutti (Italy)	Individual Points Race
Paola Pezzo (Italy)	Mountain Bike

ATHENS: 2004
Men

Chris Hoy (Great Britain)	1km. Time Trial

Chapter Five: Badminton to Cycling

Bradley Wiggins (Great Britain)	Individual Pursuit
Jens Fiedler, Stefan Nimke and Rene Wolff (Germany)	Team Sprint
Graeme Brown, Brett Lancaster, Brad McGee and Luke Roberts (Australia)	Team Pursuit
Graeme Brown and Stuart O'Grady (Australia)	Madison
Mikhail Ignatyev (Russia)	Points Race
Ryan Bailey (Australia)	Men's Sprint
Ryan Bailey (Australia)	Keiren
Paolo Bettini (Italy)	Road Race
Tyler Hamilton (USA)	Time Trial
Julien Absalon (France)	Mountain Bike

Women

Anna Meares (Australia)	500m. Time
Sarah Ulmer (New Zealand)	Individual Pursuit
Lori-Ann Muenzer (Canada)	Sprint
Olga Slyusareva (Russia)	Points Race
Sara Corrigan (Australia)	Road Race
Zijlaard-van Moorsel Leontien (Netherlands)	Time Trial
Gun-Rita Dahle (Norway)	Mountain Bike

Some Key Words and Phrases
Badminton

Battledore	Feathers	Rackets
Cork	Layout	Shuttle
Demonstration	Net	Shuttlecock

Baseball

Base	Home plate	Mound
Batter	Infield	Outfield
Diamond	Inning	Pitch

Forward to Beijing! A Guide to the Summer Olympics

Chapter Five: Badminton to Cycling

Pitcher	Player	Spin
Basketball		
Basket	Invented	Shooter
Court	Restricted area	Three-point line
Endline	Ring	Time-out
Beach volleyball		
Best-of-three	Sand	Spike
Court	Side	Time out
Round robin	Signal a serve	Two-handed
Boxing		
Bout	Headgear	Ring
Caution	Knock-out	Rounds
Combative	Random	Towel
Canoeing		
Canoe	Kayak	Rêpechage
False start	Lane	Slalom
Cycling		
BMX	Madison	Road race
Clocking	Mass start	Slipstream
Cross country	Mountain biking	Sprint
Keirin	Points race	Time trial
Lapped	Pursuit	Velodrome
General		
Croquet	Derive	Modern version
Cricket	Golf	Motor boating
Demonstration	Lacrosse	Polo

Chapter Five: Badminton to Cycling

QUIZ (badminton, baseball, basketball, beach volleyball, boxing, canoeing, cycling)

1. What game was badminton derived from?
2. When was badminton introduced as an Olympic sport?
3. In what year was cricket treated as an Olympic sport?
4. What is another name for bases in baseball?
5. On what does the pitcher stand in baseball?
6. Who is said to have invented basketball in the United States?
7. What is the maximum length of time that a basketball player whose team is in possession of the ball may spend in the opposing team's restricted area?
8. In which Olympic Games was beach volleyball introduced?
9. How many players are there in a beach volleyball Team?
10. What precautions are now taken to protect fighters in Olympic boxing?
11. In canoeing, what is the name given to a second-chance round?
12. What is a "penny farthing"?
13. What do the cyclists do in a "Madison"?
14. What building is the name "Madison" named after?
15. Where is the building that the Madison is named after?
16. What events do the following pictograms represent?

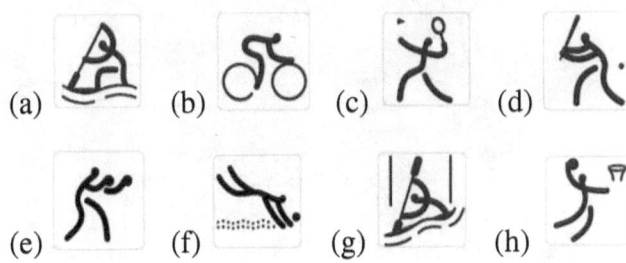

Forward to Beijing! A Guide to the Summer Olympics

Equestrian Event, Doha. *Photo Courtesy SFOCHKC.*

Chapter Six

EQUESTRIAN TO FOOTBALL (SOCCER)

Equestrian
Chariot races of different kinds and horse races played an important part in ancient athletic festivals, including the ancient Olympiad. In those days, the sport owed its origins to hunting and warfare. In the modern Olympics, chariots are no longer to be seen but horses and riders still compete against each other.

Hong Kong: Olympic City
Hong Kong SAR became an Olympic City when it was announced in July 2005 that it would be the site for all equestrian competitions in the Summer Olympics of 2008. Following the announcement, the International Olympic Committee President, Count Jacques Rogge, was invited to Hong Kong to officiate at the opening of Olympic House next to the Hong Kong Stadium and the new Olympic Square in Hong Kong Park. (This continues the tradition established in 1964 when the Colonial Governor, Sir David Trench, announced the naming of Olympic Avenue and Olympic Garden in Kowloon, commemorating the relay of Hong Kong runners who then bore the Olympic Flame through the Hong Kong streets on its way from Athens to Tokyo.)[15]

The Olympic jumping and dressage events will be held in the new Hong Kong Sports Institute situated in the town of Shatin. This venue will have a capacity for 18,000 spectators and the horses will be accommodated in four new air-conditioned stable blocks. The cross-country events will take place at the Beas River Country club and Golf Club situated in the Sheung Shui district. Both horses and riders will need to practice and facilities are being provided for such practice at Shatin Racecourse. An Equine Hospital, an Equine Clinic and a Doping Laboratory will also be established at the Racecourse.

Chapter Six: Equestrian to Football

Useful Terms: Equestrian

Dressage	Training a horse in deportment and obedience for competitions.
Courbet/ curvet	A jump forward at the levade (in Dressage).
Half Pass	Where the horse travels on a diagonal line keeping its body almost parallel with the arena wall while making forward and sideways steps in each stride.
Haute Ecole	Advanced training (in Dressage)
Levade	A movement in which the horse raises itself and stands on its bent hind legs (in Dressage).
Passage	A high-stepping trot.
Piaffe	A trot executed by the horse in place or nearly in place.
Pirouette	A 360 degree circle that is almost in place.
Oxer	A brush fence with a rail on one side.
Serpentine (in Dressage).	Half-circles performed by the horse alternately to the left and to the right while advancing.

The Rules of the Game: Equestrian

The first of several Olympic equestrian events was held in Paris in 1900. This comprised Grand Prix jumping, the High Jump and the Long Jump. The three-day event, Individual and Team (cross-country, show jumping and dressage), Team Jumping (Prix des Nations), and Individual Team Dressage have been featured every year since 1912, with the exception of the "lost" year of 1940.

Three-Day Event, Individual
This event has three parts: show-jumping, cross-country and

Chapter Six: Equestrian to Football

dressage (the training of a horse in deportment and obedience). The jumping and dressage segments observe the same rules as the regular jumping and dressage competitions. In Athens in 2004, the cross-country event consisted of a 5,700m. obstacle run that included forty-five jumping tests.

In Athens, the first disobedience at a jump was given a twenty-point penalty. A forty-point penalty was imposed for a second disobedience and elimination followed a third refusal. The first fall (if any) led to a penalty of sixty-five points. A second fall meant elimination. Penalty points were also imposed if time limits were exceeded.

Three-Day Event: Team
Only the scores of the top three finishers are counted, although each team has four members.

Jumping: Individual
Competitors who finish in the top forty-five of three qualifying rounds are able to proceed to final course A. The leading twenty in that round qualify to enter final course B. Scores earned in both rounds are added together for the results. Course A must be 600m to 700m long, with twelve obstacles and a water jump. The course should include three double jumps or one double jump and one triple jump. The obstacles must be between 1.4m and 1.6m in height. Course B must be between 500m and 600m long and differ from course A in that there are ten obstacles of varying heights from 1.4 to 1.6m. The course includes one double or one triple jump with an optional water course.

Team Jumping (Prix Des Nations)
This event consists of two rounds on a course that is 600m to 800m long with twelve to fifteen obstacles and a water jump. Each team has three or four riders and their horses. The best three scores in each round give the team score.

Chapter Six: Equestrian to Football

Dressage: Individual
The horses are made to trot and canter and walk in four different ways. Each movement is graded by five judges who take into account the submission of the horse and the position and form of the rider. The scores of the five judges are added together to determine the final score.

Dressage: Team
The scores of the top three finishers are counted, although a team can enter four riders and horses.

Gold medal winners in Equestrian events, 1988-
Winning riders' names and countries are given for individual events. The countries they represented are listed for team events.

SEOUL: 1988
Mark Todd (New Zealand)   Three-Day Event
West Germany   Three-Day Event, Team
Nicole Uphoff (West   Grand Prix (Dressage)
Germany)
Germany   Grand Prix (Dressage) Team
                                and Grand Prix (Jumping)
Pierre Durand (France)   Grand Prix Jumping

BARCELONA: 1992
Matthew Ryan (Australia)   Three-Day Event
Australia   Three-Day Event, Team
Nicole Uphoff   Grand Prix (Dressage)
Germany   Grand Prix Dressage, Team
Ludger Beerbaum   Grand Prix (Jumping)
(Germany)
The Netherlands   Grand Prix Jumping

Chapter Six: Equestrian to Football

ATLANTA: 1996
Blyth Tait (New Zealand)	Three-Day Event
Australia	Three-Day Event, Team
Isabell Werth (Germany)	Grand Prix (Dressage)
Germany	Grand Prix (Dressage), Team
Ulrich Kirchhoff (Germany)	Grand Prix (Jumping)
Germany	Grand Prix (Jumping), Team

SYDNEY: 2000
David O'Conner (USA)	Three-Day Event.
Australia	Three-Day Event, Team
Anky van Grunsven (Netherlands)	Grand Prix (Dressage)
Germany	Grand Prix (Dressage) Team
Jeroen Dubbeldam (Netherlands)	Grand Prix (Jumping)
Germany	Grand Prix (Jumping) Team
Anky van Grunsven (Netherlands)	Individual Dressage Freestyle to Music

ATHENS: 2004
Leslie Law (Great Britain)	Three Day Event
France	Three-Day Event, Team
Germany	Team Event (Dressage)
Germany	Team Event (Jumping)
Anky van Grunsven (Netherlands)	Individual Dressage
Anky van Grunsven (Netherlands)	Individual Jumping

Fencing

Fencing originated in ancient times when swords of different sizes and weights were used in combat. Sometimes, the skillful use of a sword according to established movements and rules was practiced as a pastime. Modern fencing sprang from unarmed

Chapter Six: Equestrian to Football

duelling contests with rapiers. These lightweight swords were used to thrust at opponents to pierce, rather than to cut. Prior to the 1980s fencing was the only Olympic sport that allowed professionals to compete. The individual foil event for men was held first at the 1896 Olympics. Team foil competitions were added in 1904 but these were suspended until 1920. Foil contests for women were introduced first at the 1924 Olympics.

In the Olympic fencing competition today, three types of sword are used: the foil, the épée and the sabre.

Useful Terms: Fencing

Appel	Stamping or beating of the foot in a competition.
Bout	A contest in its entirety between two fencers.
Epée	A sword which is heavier than a foil.
Fleche	A running attack.
Foil	A long, thin, light sword which normally has a circular guard and a flexible blade with a button on the tip.
Hit	A point scored by a touch with the tip of the blade or, in sabre competitions, the edge of the blade against any part of the opponent's body in the target area.
Piste	The area in which a fencing competition is held.
Touche	Acknowledging a scoring hit by an opponent in a contest.
Victory	Winning a bout.

The Rules of the Game: Fencing

Fencing bouts are held on a "piste", that is an area marked with a central line. On-guard lines, rear lines and colour zones indicate

Chapter Six: Equestrian to Football

the areas close to out-of-limits zones. If a fencer enters an out-of-limits zone, a point is awarded to the opponent.

Any hit with a foil must be made on the trunk of the body; touches with the épée can be made on any part of the body and touches with the sabre may only be made on the body above the waist, including the arms and the head.

There are six fencing events for men and four for women. The individual foil event for men was held first in 1896. Team foil was added in 1904 but then suspended until 1920. The individual épée event was introduced in 1900 and the team épée event in 1906. The individual sabre competition began in 1896 and the team sabre event started in 1906.

The individual foil event for women was first held in 1924 in Paris. The individual épée event was introduced in 1996, together with the team épée event. An individual sabre event was held for the first time in Athens in 2004.

Each team has three members with the first to score a total of forty-five hits declared the winner. A hit is worth one point and a light shines on an electronically controlled board indicating who has struck. The first bout ends when a team reaches five points. The second bout finishes at ten points, the third when fifteen points is reached and so on until forty-five points have been scored or nine bouts completed, whichever comes first. In the event of a tie after nine minutes, an additional "sudden-death" overtime period of one minute is introduced.

Gold medal winners in Fencing, 1988-
Winning athletes' names and countries are given for individual events. The countries they represented are listed for team events.

1988: SEOUL
Men
Stefano Cerioni (Italy)   Individual foil

Chapter Six: Equestrian to Football

USSR	Team Foil
Jean-Francois Lanour (France)	Individual Sabre
Hungary	Team Sabre
Arnd Schmidt (West Germany)	Individual Épée
France	Team Épée competition
Women	
Anja Fichtel (West Germany)	Individual Foil
Germany	Team Foil

BARCELONA: 1992
Men

Philippe Omnes (France)	Individual Foil
Germany	Team Foil
Benco Szabo (Hungary)	Individual Sabre
Unified Team	Team Sabre
Eric Stecki (France)	Individual Épée
Germany	Team Épée
Women	
Giovanna Trillini (Italy)	Individual Foil
Italy	Team Foil

ATLANTA: 1996
Men

Alexandro Puccini (Italy)	Individual Foil
Russia	Team Foil
Alexander Beketov (Russia)	Individual Épée
Italy	Team Épée
Sergei Podnyakov (Russia)	Individual Sabre
Russia	Team Sabre
Women	
Laura Badea (Romania)	Individual Foil

Chapter Six: Equestrian to Football

Italy	Team Foil
Laura Flessel (France)	Individual Épée
France	Team Épée

SYDNEY: 2000
Men

Pavel Kolobkov (Russia)	Individual Épée
Italy	Team Épée
Young-Ho Kim (Korea)	Individual Foil
France	Team Foil
Mihai Claudiu Covaliu (Romania)	Individual Sabre
Russia	Team Sabre

Women

Timea Nagy (Hungary)	Individual Épée
Russia	Team Épée
Valentina Vezzali (Italy)	Individual Foil
Italy	Team Foil

2004: ATHENS
Men

Montano Aldo (Italy)	Individual Sabre
France	Team Sabre
Guyard Brice (France)	Individual Foil
Italy	Team Foil
Marcel Fischer (Switzerland)	Individual Épée
France	Team Épée

Women

Nagy Timea (Hungary)	Individual Épée
Russia	Team Épée
Zagunis Mariel (United States)	Individual Sabre
Vezzali Valentina (Italy)	Individual Foil

Chapter Six: Equestrian to Football

Football (Soccer)

Football (Soccer) for men, not to be confused with American football, was introduced into the Olympic Games in 1900 and 1904 as an exhibition sport and it later became the first team sport to be included. Football has been part of every Olympiad, except the 1932 Games in Los Angeles, where it might have been confused with American Football. Women's events were added to the programme in 1996.

There are convincing similarities between the game invented in England and the game, "tsu chu", played in China in the third century B.C. This involved kicking a pigskin ball between goal posts made of bamboo. The Greeks are said to have copied this Chinese game and it was later adopted by the Romans and other European countries.

Modern terms in football are different from those used in the recent past. The new terms reflect changes in strategy and tactics. The modern terms, "striker", "sweeper", and "defender" were never used in the past. The titles given to the players were: Goalkeeper, Left Fullback, Right Fullback, Left Half, Centre Half, Right Half; Outside Left, Inside Left, Centre Forward, Inside Right and Outside Right.

Useful Terms: Football (soccer)

Banana kick	A kick that gives the ball a curved trajectory
Carrying the ball	A foul committed by the goalkeeper if he/she takes more than four steps while holding or bouncing the ball.
Catenaccio	A defensive system employing a "sweeper".
Goal line	The two shorter boundary lines on which the goal stands, marking each end of the field of play.
Golden goal	The first goal scored during extra time.
Offside	A violation in which a player is closer to the

Chapter Six: Equestrian to Football

	opponents' goal line than any defenders except the goalkeeper when receiving a pass.
Striker	An attacking player in a well forward position from which to score goals. (Formerly centre-forward.)
Sweeper	A player who plays behind the central defenders. He or she provides extra defence but also looks for opportunities to create attacking play.
Wall Pass	A pass around a defender to another player.
Yellow card	A card that the referee holds up to warn a player for unsportsmanlike or dangerous behaviour.

The Rules of the Game: Football (soccer)

It seems superfluous to offer a description of football since the game is understood and followed by millions of people worldwide, thanks to television coverage. There are, however, some rules which are peculiar to the Olympic version. Olympic football must be played on natural turf. Substitutions are allowed, but no more than two in a match. Each match consists of two forty-five minute halves. If play is halted because of injury to a player, then the time lost is added to the end of each half. In the eliminating rounds, a thirty minute overtime period is allowed, if needed. A "sudden death" overtime period is also possible. The first team to score in overtime is declared the winner. If the score is still tied after 120 minutes, then the match is decided by a penalty shoot-out, five against five.

In 2004, the men's tournament featured sixteen teams and the women's tournament ten teams. For the 2008 Games, the number of women's teams has been increased to twelve. The men's tournament is set at sixteen teams, as was the case in 2004.

Chapter Six: Equestrian to Football

Gold medal winning teams in Football (soccer), 1988-

Seoul: 1988 USSR	Barcelona: 1992 Spain	Atlanta: 1996 **Men** Nigeria **Women** USA
Sydney: 2000 **Men** Cameroon **Women** Norway:	Athens: 2004 **Men** Argentina **Women** USA	Beijing: 2008 **Men** .... **Women** ....

Some Key Words and Phrases
Equestrian
Canter
Deportment
Disobedience
Dressage
Hind Legs

Obstacle
Refusal
Triple Jump
Trot
Water Jump

Fencing
Blade
Button
Épée
Foil

Guard
Piste
Sabre
Sudden Death

Football (soccer)
Attacker
Boundary
Defender
Injury
Overtime

Shoot-out
Substitution
Touch
Turf
Violation

Chapter Six: Equestrian to Football

QUIZ (equestrian, fencing, football (soccer))

1. Where and when were the first equestrian events held?
2. How many parts are there in the three-day individual equestrian event?
3. How many rounds are there in the team jumping event?
4. What do the horses have to do in the individual dressage event?
5. How are events in fencing distinguished from each other?
6. Where was the first women's individual foil event held?
7. When was soccer first included in the Olympic Games?
8. When was women's soccer introduced into the Games?
9. What is the length of a soccer match at the Olympic Games?
10. What is the name of the ancient Chinese game that was similar to soccer?
11. What is a "golden goal"?
12. How many men's soccer teams may compete in the 2008 Olympics?
13. What is the maximum number of substitutions allowed in Olympic soccer?
14. What was the former name given to a "striker" in soccer?
15. Which events do the following pictograms represent?

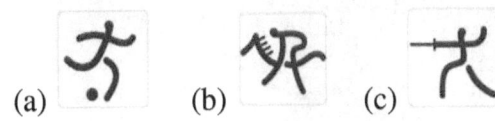

(a)   (b)   (c)

Women's Hockey, Doha Asian Games, December 2007. *Photo Courtesy SFOCHKC.*

CHAN Ka Man (L). Women's Judo, Doha Asian Games, December 2007. *Photo Courtesy SFOCHKC.* ~ Important in themselves, these Games were a good preparation and selection tool for the Beijing Summer Olympics, 2008.

Chapter Seven

GYMNASTICS TO JUDO

Gymnastics
The word "gymnastics" is derived from the Greek word, "gymnos", meaning "naked". When gymnastics began in ancient Greece more than 2,000 years ago, the gymnasium was a centre of cultural activity where men gathered together to discuss music, art and philosophy, but also to exercise for health reasons, usually in minimal dress. Most Greek cities had gymnasia, places where running, wrestling and jumping exercises could be practised. The movements involved in such exercises required balance, flexibility, endurance and physical strength.

World-wide interest in organised physical exercises waned after Emperor Theodosius abolished the Olympic Games, but there was something of a revival in Germany in the eighteenth and nineteenth centuries when two physical education practitioners, Friedrich Ludwig Jahn (1778-1852) and Friedrich Gutsmuth (1759-1839), designed apparatus which young men could use for different types of exercise. Updated versions of this apparatus (for example, parallel bars) are still in use today.

Followers of Jahn's methods in the United States made use of his apparatus to develop callisthenics: exercises to develop bodily fitness and grace of movement.

Sporting activities such as Rugby and cross-country running were introduced in British Public Schools in the nineteenth century and, amongst the public at large, horse-racing and "fisticuffs" (without gloves) became popular. In the early twentieth century, the "Keep Fit" movement featuring "physical jerks" (performed in fitness classes) proved to be very successful in British holiday camps.

A gymnastic competition was included in the first Olympics held in 1896, including exercises such as rope climbing,

Chapter Seven: Gymnastics to Judo

club swinging, tumbling and the "Swedish System", each now discontinued. By 1954, Olympic events and apparatus had been standardized and a new points system introduced.

Nowadays, the Olympic gymnastics event has three disciplines: artistic gymnastics, rhythmic gymnastics and trampoline. The first all-round competition for artistic gymnastics was introduced in the Paris Games in 1900. The rhythmic individual all-round competition was added in 1984. The trampoline event is relatively new and was included for the first time in Sydney in 2000.

Useful Terms: Gymnastics

Arab spring	A "cartwheel" with a quarter turn.
Buck	A vaulting "horse".
Compulsories	Pre-designed routines requiring specific movements from all competitors.
Hecht	Dismounting the exercise bars with the head and body first between the bars.
Kip	Straightening the body by pushing the legs back and the hips forward.
Planche	The body is horizontal, facing downwards and is supported by straight arms above the apparatus.
Pommel Horse	A vaulting "horse" fitted with two handgrips.
Salto	A flip or somersault with the feet coming over the head and the body rotating around the axis of the waist.
Tkachyov	A 360-degree swing on a horizontal bar.
Tsukahara	A vault made with a half or quarter turn onto the pommel horse, followed by one and a half somersaults off the horse.

Chapter Seven: Gymnastics to Judo

The Rules of the Game (Gymnastics)

Artistic Gymnastics

In artistic gymnastics, men compete in floor exercises and on various types of apparatus including the pommel horse, rings, parallel bars and the horizontal bar. Women compete in the vault, on uneven bars, on balance beams and in floor exercises. There are individual all-round contests, apparatus finals and team competitions.

In the past, each gymnast had to perform, first, compulsory exercises and, second, optional exercises on each apparatus. However, in the 2000 Olympics, the compulsory exercises were eliminated. Following additional new rules introduced in the 2004 Athens Olympics, two gymnasts from each competing country took part in the all-round final. In the team competition, the top eight athletes qualified for the apparatus finals. Two judges assessed the degree of difficulty — the "start value" — of each routine and six other judges awarded scores for execution. The lowest and highest marks were then ruled out and an average of the four remaining marks was subtracted from the start value, to determine the final score of each competitor.

MEN
Vault
Competitors hurdle onto a spring board and then rotate to a standing position. Multiple twists and somersaults are usually added. Success depends on the length of the hurdle, the speed of the run and the speed of rotation.

The horizontal bars
In the horizontal bar competition, the bar is 2.5m long, standing 2.55m above the ground.

Chapter Seven: Gymnastics to Judo

The parallel bars
These are 1.95m high and 3.5m long. Their distance apart is between 42cm and 52cm. The contestants must perform a series of balances, swings and releases.

The Pommel Horse
This is 1.15m high, 35cm wide and 1.6m long. The distance between the pommels is between 40cm and 45cm. The competitors must carry out continuous circular movements around the horse while allowing only their hands to touch it.

The Rings
The rings are made of wood and are hung 2.8m above a mat. Contestants must engage in a routine that demonstrates strength and balance while making sure that the rings themselves do not swing.

Floor exercises
For men, these exercises must last between fifty and seventy seconds. They must include one backward and one forward tumble and a balancing feature on one leg or arm.

Team combined exercises
Each team has six competitors. Three of these perform each group of exercises. Final scores are derived by combining the scores of the top five gymnasts. Twelve teams participate in a qualifying round and the leading eight move up to the final.

WOMEN
Side Horse Vault
In this event, women vault from the side of the horse, whereas men vault across the length. The horse is 1.2m high and 1.63m long. Women may have two attempts and the scores are averaged to reach a final score.

Chapter Seven: Gymnastics to Judo

Uneven (Asymmetric) Bars
The two parallel bars are 3.5m long. The high bar must be between 2.2m and 2.4m above the floor. The low bar must be between 1.4m and 1.6m above the floor. The contestants perform circling, swinging and handstands on the bars.

Balance Beam
The beam must be 5m long and 10cm wide. It must stand 1.2m above the floor. The competitors perform turns, leaps and dance movements.

Floor Exercises
Contestants perform exercises to music. These include jumps, turns and passes.

Team Combined Exercises
Each country's final score is calculated by combining the scores of the top five performers on each apparatus.

Rhythmic Gymnastics

Rhythmic All-Round
At present this competition is only open to women who use different accessories in routines that last from seventy-five to ninety seconds. At the Athens Olympics, the accessories were ribbon, clubs, balls and hoops. Each performance was scored by ten judges, five for execution and five for composition.

Rhythmic Team
At the Athens Olympics, two sets of accessories were used, one set of five ribbons and the other set of three hoops and two balls. There were six members in each national team. Ten teams competed, the top six teams moving up to the final.

Chapter Seven: Gymnastics to Judo

Trampoline
At present, only individual trampoline is included in the Olympics. The contestant jumps to achieve height followed by a sequence of ten leaps during which he or she performs a number of tumbling skills.

Sixteen men and sixteen women took part in the 2004 Olympics. The leading eight competitors were determined in a qualifying round. These competitors moved up to the final at which each was asked to perform ten different moves. Five judges awarded points for execution; two judges gave one score for degree of difficulty and two were in overall control of the judging. The lowest and highest execution scores were ignored and the remaining three scores were added to the one score given for difficulty.

Gold medal winners in Gymnastics, 1988-
Winning athletes' names and countries are given for individual events. The countries they represented are listed for team events.

SEOUL: 1988
Men

Vladimir Artemov (Soviet Union)	Individual Combined Exercises
USSR	Team
Vladimir Artemov (Soviet Union)	Parallel Bars
Sergei Kharkov (Soviet Union)	Floor
Lou Yun (China)	Horse Vault
Vladimir Artemov (Soviet Union)	Horizontal Bar
Valerie Lukin (Soviet Union)	Horizontal Bar
Holger Behrendt (East Germany)	Rings

112   Forward to Beijing! A Guide to the Summer Olympics

Chapter Seven: Gymnastics to Judo

Dimitri Biloserchev (Soviet Union)	Rings
Lubomir Gueraskol (Bulgaria)	Pommel Horse
Zsolt Borkai (Hungary)	Pommel Horse
Dimitri Biloserchev (Soviet Union)	Pommel Horse

Women

Elena Shushunova (Soviet Union)	Individual Combined Exercises
USSR	Team
Daniela Silivas (Romania)	Floor
Svetlana Boginskaya (Soviet Union)	Horse Vault
Daniela Silivas (Romania)	Beam
Daniela Silivas (Romania)	Asymmetrical Bars
Marina Lobach (Soviet Union)	Modern Rhythmic

BARCELONA: 1992
Men

Vitali Sherbo (Unified Team)	Individual Combined Exercises
Unified Team	Individual Team
Vitali Sherbo (Unified Team)	Parallel Bars
Li Jing (China)	Parallel Bars
Li Xiaoahuang (China)	Floor
Vitali Sherbo (Unified Team)	Horse Vault
Trent Dimas (USA)	Horizontal Bar
Vitali Sherbo (Unified Team)	Rings
Vitali Sherbo (Unified Team)	Pommel Horse

Women

Tatyana Gutsu (Unified Team)	Individual Combined Exercises

Chapter Seven: Gymnastics to Judo

Unified Team	Team
Lavinia Milosovici (Romania)	Floor
Henrietta Onodi (Hungary)	Horse Vault
Tatyana Lyssenko (Unified Team)	Beam
Li Lu (China)	Asymmetrical Bars
Alexandra Timoshenko (Unified Team)	Modern Rhythmic

SYDNEY: 2000
Men

Alexei Nemov (Russia)	Individual Combined Exercises
China (Wei Yang, Lihui Zheng, Xiaopeng Li, Aowei Xing, Xu Huang, Junfeng Xiao)	Team
Li Xiaopeng (China)	Parallel Bars
Igor Vihrovs (Lithuania)	Floor
Gervasio Deferr (Spain)	Horse Vault
Alexei Nemov (Russia)	Horizontal Bar
Szilveszter Csollany (Hungary)	Rings
Marius Daniel Urzica (Romania)	Pommel Horse
Alexandre Moskalenko (Russia)	Trampoline

Women

Simona Amanar (Romania)	Individual Combined Exercises
Romania	Team
Elena Zamolodtchikova (Russia)	Floor

Chapter Seven: Gymnastics to Judo

Elena Zamolodtchikova (Russia)	Horse Vault
Liu Xuan (China)	Beam
Svetlana Khorkina (Russia)	Asymmetrical Bars
Yulia Barsukova (Russia)	Rhythmic Individual
Russia	Rhythmic Team
Irina Karavaeva (Russia)	Trampoline

ATHENS: 2004
Men

Paul Hamm (USA)	Individual All Round
Japan	Team Competition
Kyle Shewfelt (Canada)	Floor Exercise
Japan	Team Floor
Deferr Gervasio (Spain)	Horse Vault
Igor Cassina (Italy)	Horizontal Bar
Tampakos Dimosthenis (Greece)	Rings
Teng Haibin (China)	Pommel Horse
Nikitin Yuri (Ukraine)	Trampoline
Valeri Goncharov	Parallel Bars

Women

Carly Patterson (USA)	Individual All Round
Monica Rosu (Romania)	Horse Vault
Emilie Lepennec (France)	Asymmetrical Bars
Catalina Ponor (Romania)	Balance Beam
Catalina Ponor (Romania)	Floor Exercise
Romania	Team Competition
Kabaeva Alina (Russia)	Rhythmic All Round
Russia	Rhythmic Group Competition
Dogonadze Anna (Germany)	Trampoline

Chapter Seven: Gymnastics to Judo

Handball (Team)
Handball seems to have been played in Greece at least as early as 600BC. It continued to be played in various forms throughout the centuries and there are accounts of it being played in Ireland from the year 1700. Immigrants took the one-wall game with them from Ireland to England and the game gained popularity in that form.

Men's handball was added to the Olympic programme in 1936 when a competition involving sixteen men's teams was staged. It featured then as an outdoor sport. After 1936 it was not included again until the Munich Games in 1972 when it was transformed into an indoor sport. Women's handball was introduced four years later at the 1976 Olympic Games held in Montreal.

Twelve teams took part in the 2004 Athens Olympics. The teams were divided into two sections and the four leading teams from each section advanced to the semi-finals.

Useful Terms: Handball

Centre back	A player who is centred largely around mid-court and who shoots when possible to try to penetrate the defence.
Field players	The players on the court (except the goalkeeper), also known as court players.
Goal area	A D-shaped area extending six metres from the goal and occupied only by the goalkeeper.
Jump shot	A shot attempted while leaping.
One-wall handball	Involves striking a rubber ball against a wall in such a way that the opponent is unable to return it.
Team Handball	Quite different from "one-wall handball".

Chapter Seven: Gymnastics to Judo

Throw-off   The referee throws the ball in the air at the start of the game.

The Rules of the Game: Handball

Handball is a fast-paced sport similar to basketball, except that the aim is to throw the ball into a goal past a goalkeeper, rather than land the ball in a net. Only the goalkeeper may enter the goal area, although a shooter may start outside the area and jump towards the goal provided that he shoots before landing on the floor. This is known as a "jump shot".

Divided into two thirty-minute halves, the game is played by teams of seven field players a side, on a court measuring 20m by 40m. Different formations can be seen in handball. Whatever the formation, however, there is always a goalkeeper whose aim is to keep out balls that are thrown at him. A typical formation is to have players at the left, right and centre of the court, stationed there because they are usually proficient at high jumps and shooting over the defenders. A centre player often intermingles with the defence to try to disrupt its formation. Another centre may have the role of "playmaker", always alert to the possibility of scoring. His job is to move the ball up the court to break down the opponents' defence. The seventh player is called a "circle runner" and plays a free defending and attacking role around the court.

A player may take three steps only, either before, or after, dribbling with the ball, but he or she may not hold the ball for more than three seconds without passing it to one of the other six players in the team. Goals can be scored into an area that is two metres high and three metres wide. The net at the base of the goal must be one metre deep.

A handball is normally made of leather, weighing between 425kg and 481kg with a circumference of 58.4cm-61cm. The ball used by women should weigh between 340kg and 396kg and have

Chapter Seven: Gymnastics to Judo

a circumference of 53.3cm-55.9cm.

A seven metre throw is awarded when a player has been fouled during a shot. The throw must be taken from the seven metre line, with only the goalkeeper between the goal and the shooter.

A handball game is divided into two thirty-minute halves. In the 2004 Athens Olympics, twelve teams took part.

Gold medal winning teams in Handball, 1988-

	Men	Women
Seoul: 1988	USSR	South Korea
Barcelona: 1992	The Unified Team	South Korea
Atlanta: 1996	Croatia	Denmark
Sydney: 2000	Russia	Denmark
Athens: 2004	Croatia	Denmark
Beijing: 2008	....	....
London: 2012	....	....

Hockey (Field Hockey)
The word "hockey" ("hockie") is said to date from the 16th century and to have become an organized game at the end of the 19th century. There is, however, evidence that a form of the game was known to much earlier civilizations. Dating from about 2000BC, a drawing on an Egyptian tomb depicts two men standing near a ball and holding curved sticks. A similar drawing, but showing six players, was discovered in Greece dating from about 500BC.

Men's hockey was added to the Olympic programme in 1908 but it was not until the 1980 Moscow Games that women's hockey became an Olympic sport.

Chapter Seven: Gymnastics to Judo

Useful Terms: Hockey (Field Hockey)

Bully	A method of re-starting play following a stoppage not caused by a breach. Two players face each other, standing close. Together, they tap their sticks on the ground and against each other's sticks before contesting the ball.
Dribble	To move the ball while controlling it with a stick.
Field Hockey	This term is used to distinguish the game from ice hockey.
Free Hit	A passing opportunity awarded to a player for any offence by the opposition outside the circle.
Penalty corners	Free hits awarded to a team ten metres from the nearest goalpost, allowing players to pass the ball to a team-mate just outside the goal circle.
Stick	A curved wooden stick, 90cm to 96cm long. Today, sticks are also made of fibreglass and other man-made materials.
Striking areas	The D-shaped areas in front of the goals, which an attacking player must enter before shooting at goal.
Face-off	Same as bully-off. This action starts a game. (See below.)

The Rules of the Game: Hockey (Field Hockey)

Today, field hockey is a ball game involving two competing teams. Each team has eleven players, including a goalkeeper. Using hooked sticks to propel the ball, players in each team attempt to direct the ball past the opposing side's goalkeeper and

Chapter Seven: Gymnastics to Judo

into the goal. This goal must be 2.13m high and 3.66m wide.

The game is divided into two 35-minute halves and extra time can be added if there is a delay because of injury to a player.

Hockey sticks are flat on one side and curved on the other. Only the flat side may be used to propel the ball. Players must not touch the ball with any part of their bodies, including their hands. All shots aimed at the goals can only be made from striking areas that extend in semi-circles 14.6m from each goal.

Hockey includes a "bully" that starts each game. The ball is placed on the ground between two players, one from each team. Each of these two players taps the ground once with his stick. Then both players tap each other's sticks, before trying to take possession of the ball and directing it towards their opponents' goal. Points are scored by hitting the ball between the opposite side's goalposts.

Penalties can be declared (usually a free hit to the other side) for kicking or throwing the ball, playing without holding the stick, striking with the rounded side of the stick and interfering with an opponent's stick. Penalty corners can be awarded for an offence committed inside a 23m line or if the ball has been deliberately propelled over the goal line.

In Olympic hockey, the top two teams in preliminary matches move up to semi-finals. Ten teams compete in the women's tournament and twelve teams face each other in the men's tournament.

Gold medal winning teams in Hockey (Field Hockey), 1988-

	Men	Women
Seoul: 1988	Great Britain	Australia
Barcelona: 1992	Germany	Spain
Atlanta: 1996	The Netherlands	Australia
Sydney: 2000	The Netherlands	Australia
Athens: 2004	Australia	Germany

Chapter Seven: Gymnastics to Judo

Beijing: 2008   …………..   …………..
London: 2012   …………..   …………..

Judo

Judo ("the gentle way") is one of the best known forms of the *bujutsu* (martial arts). It aims at cultivating the mind and training the body through different methods of defence and attack. The emphasis is placed on yielding to an opponent's strength rather than attempting to defeat him by force. This version of wrestling was developed in Japan in the late 19th century by Professor Jigoro Kano. It has its origins in military "jujutsu", a hand-to-hand combat technique practiced originally by samurai warriors in Japan and refined by Chinese ideas of chivalry and fair play in the thirteenth century.

Men's Judo was added to the Olympic Games programme in 1964, in Tokyo. Although Japan triumphed in the lightweight, middleweight and heavyweight Judo contests with sixteen gold medals, the gold medal in the prestigious open category went to Antonius Geesink of the Netherlands, a two metre tall instructor from Utrecht. The open event was discontinued in 1984 after the Games held in Los Angeles.

Women's Judo was added to the programme in 1992, at Barcelona.

Useful Terms: Judo
The terms used in Judo are derived from Japanese words.

Chui	A warning incurring a penalty of five points.
Hansoku Make	The highest penalty warning, meriting disqualification.
Ippon	A match-winning throw or hold scoring ten points.
Judogi	A Judo suit.
Judoka	A Judo player.

Chapter Seven: Gymnastics to Judo

Katame-waza	A basic hold.
Keikosu	A warning incurring a penalty of seven points.
Kinsa	An advantage (worth three points).
Koka	A hold that lasts between ten and twenty seconds.
Mata	Breaking a hold.
Nage-Waza	A name for throwing techniques (in general).
Shido	A warning by a judge. No points are deducted.
Shime-waza	A strangulation technique.
Wazari	A throw that almost lands an opponent on his or her back (worth seven points).
Wazari-ni-chikai-waza	A partial hold or throw. Two of these make an ippon (worth five points).
Yuko	A hold that lasts between twenty and twenty-five seconds (worth five points).

The Rules of the Game: Judo

As in boxing and wrestling, the athletes in Judo are separated according to their weight but in different categories. There are currently seven weight classes for both men and women. Contestants compete with opponents in their own weight class. Each weight division is split into two pools. The combatants then fight a single elimination tournament. Each of the two pool winners compete for the gold medal and the loser is awarded a silver medal. Competitors who lose to the finalists compete in another single elimination round in each of the two pools. The winner of each pool faces the runner-up in the opposing pool. The last two winners take the two bronze medals.

The Judo bouts take place on tatami mats, made of layers

Chapter Seven: Gymnastics to Judo

of rushes and usually edged with black cloth. A match takes place in an area that measures fourteen metres by fourteen metres.

Contestants known as *judoka* wear loose-fitting white clothes named *judogis*, consisting of trousers, a jacket and a coloured belt. An *ippon* ends the match. This is when a combatant scores points by forcing an opponent onto his or her back for thirty seconds, or successfully applies a strangle or choke or a lock against the elbow, or executes a forceful, clean throw. Other points can be earned by throws (*waza-ari*, *yuko* and *koka*). These count towards a total, but are not good enough for *ippon*.

A *judoka* will be disqualified if he receives four warnings within a match.

All men's matches last for five minutes. Women's matches last for four minutes.

Contestants may not go to the floor deliberately, strike an opponent or carry out a fake attack. Trying to injure an opponent, leaving the tatami deliberately, using overly defensive tactics or disobeying the judges are also prohibited by the rules.

Six officials — two judges, two time-keepers, a referee and a list writer (a person who records the development of a contest) — control judo matches.

Note: Women entered for the Judo competition for the first time in 1992.

Gold medal winners in Judo, 1988-

SEOUL: 1988
Kim Jae Yup (Korea)	Super Lightweight
Lee Kyung Keun (Korea)	Half-Lightweight
Marc Alexandre (France)	Lightweight
Waldemar Legien (Poland)	Light Middleweight
Peter Seisenbacher (Austria)	Middleweight
Aurelio Miguel (Brazil)	Light-Heavyweight

Chapter Seven: Gymnastics to Judo

Hitoshi Saito (Japan)	Heavyweight

BARCELONA: 1992
Men

Nazim Gusseinov (Unified Team)	Super-Lightweight
Rogerio Sampaio Cardoso (Brazil)	Half-Lightweight
Toshihiko Koga (Japan)	Lightweight
Hidehiko Yoshida (Japan)	Light Middleweight
Waldemar Legien (Poland)	Middleweight
Antal Kovacs (Hungary)	Light Heavyweight
David Shashaleshvili (Unified Team)	Heavyweight

Women

Cecile Novak (France)	Super-Lightweight
Almudena Munoz (Spain)	Half-Lightweight
Miriam Blasco (Spain)	Lightweight
Catherine Fleury (France)	Light-Middleweight
Odalis Reve Jimenez (Cuba)	Middleweight
Kim Mi-Jung (Korea)	Light-Heavyweight
Zhuang Xiaoyan (China)	Heavyweight

ATLANTA: 1996
Men

Tadahiro Nomura (Japan)	Super-Lightweight
Udo Quellmalz (Germany)	Half-Lightweight
Kenzo Nakamura (Japan)	Lightweight
Djamel Bouras (France)	Light-Middleweight
Jeon Ki-young (Korea)	Middleweight
Pawel Nastula (Poland)	Light-Heavyweight
David Douillet (France)	Heavyweight

Women

Kye Sun (North Korea)	Super Lightweight

Chapter Seven: Gymnastics to Judo

Marie-Claire Restoux (France)	Half-Lightweight
Driulis Gonzalez Morales (Cuba)	Lightweight
Yuko Emoto (Japan)	Light-Middleweight
Cho Min-Sun (Korea)	Middleweight
Ulla Werbrouck (Hungary)	Light-Heavyweight
Sun Fu-Ming (China)	Heavyweight

SYDNEY: 2000
Men

Tadahiro Nomura (Japan)	Super Lightweight *Repeating his success in Atlanta.*
Huseyin Ozkan (Turkey)	Half-Lightweight
Giuseppe Maddaloni (Italy)	Lightweight
Makoto Takimoto (Japan)	Half-Middleweight
Mark Huizinga (Netherlands)	Middleweight
Kosei Inoue (Japan)	Half-Heavyweight
David Douillet (France)	Heavyweight *Repeating his success in Atlanta.*

Women

Ryoko Tamura (Japan)	Super-Lightweight
Legna Verdecia (Cuba)	Half-Lightweight
Isabel Fernandez (Spain)	Lightweight
Severine Vandenhende (France)	Half-Middleweight
Sibelis Veranes (Cuba)	Middleweight
Lin Tang (China)	Half Heavyweight
Hua Yuan (China)	Heavyweight

ATHENS: 2004
Men

Tadahiro Nomura (Japan).	60kg *Successful again in his third Olympics.*

Chapter Seven: Gymnastics to Judo

Uchishiba Masato (Japan)	66kg
Lee Won Hee (Korea)	73kg
Iliadis Ilias (Greece)	81kg
Zviadauri Zurab (Georgia)	90kg
Makarau Ihar (Belarus)	100kg
Suzuki Keiji (Japan)	100+kg
Women	
Ryoko Tani (formerly Tamura)	48kg
Xian Dongmei (China)	52kg
Boenisch Yvonne (Germany)	57kg
Tanimoto Ayumi (Japan)	63kg
Ueno Masae (Japan)	70kg
Anno Noriko (Japan)	78kg
Tsukada Maki (Japan)	78+kg

Some Key Words
Gymnastics

Apparatus	Horizontal Bar	Pommel Horse
Asymmetrical	Horse Vault	Rhythmic
Bars	Optional	Rings
Beam	Parallel Bars	Trampoline

Handball

Circle runner	One-wall	Team
Goal-keeper	Playmaker	Throw off
Jump-shot	Shoot	Transformed

Hockey

Bully	Face off	Penalty corner
Dribble	Free hit	Stick

Judo

Category	Combat	Hand to hand
Chivalry	Fair play	Technique

Chapter Seven: Gymnastics to Judo

QUIZ (gymnastics, handball, hockey (field hockey), judo)

1. When were floor exercises introduced for the first time in the Olympic Games?
2. When were compulsory exercises eliminated from the Olympic Gymnastics event?
3. What is another term for "the degree of difficulty"?
4. Name two of the "accessories" used by women in the rhythmic all-round event in gymnastics.
5. When did handball become an Olympic sport for women?
6. How many players are there in a field hockey team?
7. What are "tatami" mats made of?
8. How are the athletes separated into classes in Judo?
9. What brings a Judo match to an end?
10. How long does a women's Judo match last?
11. What events do the following pictograms represent?

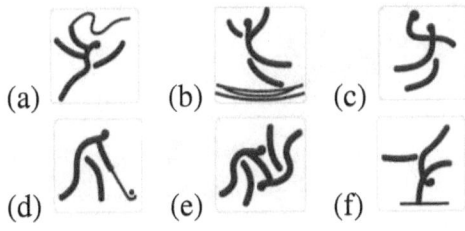

(a)   (b)   (c)   (d)   (e)   (f)

Lee Lai Shan, "Queen of the Wind". Hong Kong's only Olympic gold medal winner during the period of its British administration. Women's Mistral event (wind-surfing), Athens Summer Olympics, 2004. *Photo Courtesy SFOCHKC.*

Chapter Eight

MODERN PENTATHLON TO SOFTBALL

Modern Pentathlon
The modern pentathlon was introduced as an Olympic sport upon the suggestion of Baron de Coubertin. Pierre de Courbertin envisaged a competition that would identify the greatest all-round sportsman. Although he believed that his modern version could match the pentathlon of the ancient Greek Games, the two versions have, from the start, resembled each other only in name. The ancient event took place in a single day and comprised running, wrestling, jumping, discus and javelin throwing. The discuses that have been excavated in Greece were made of stone or metal. This guaranteed their survival over many centuries. No javelins have lasted because they were made of wood. We do, however, know what they looked like through artistic evidence, for example paintings on ancient vases.

A puzzle that has still to be satisfactorily solved is why Greek athletes carried weights when they jumped. Perhaps this was an early form of handicapping.

The modern pentathlon event took place over five days at the Olympic Games held from 1912 to 1980. At the Atlanta Games in 1996, however, the pentathlon began to look more like the Games of old by being compressed into a single day.

Accounts of the origins of the modern pentathlon exist in several versions. Most agree that the choice of five apparently unrelated sports is linked to a fable about the adventures of a young French cavalry officer in the 19th century. His *horse* is shot in enemy territory. Leaving his mount, he defends himself with his *sword* and *pistol*, *swims* across a river and triumphantly *runs* to deliver the message with which he has been entrusted.

The modern competition is not for the faint-hearted or the inadequately prepared. It begins at 7.30am with pistol shooting.

Chapter Eight: Modern Pentathlon to Softball

This is followed by fencing at about 10am, swimming at 1pm and horse riding at 2pm. A cross-country running event is added at 6pm.
    The sport was added to the women's Olympic programme in Sydney in 2000.

Useful Terms: Modern Pentathlon

Air pistols	Short firearms that use compressed air or carbon dioxide to discharge lead pellets.
Cross-country	A race that is run across mostly rough terrain, as opposed to a pristine track.
Obstacles	Objects that horses must clear to complete a course, such as fences, gates or water jumps.
Pentathlete	A competitor who enters for the modern pentathlon event.
Refusal	A horse's act of stopping in front of an obstacle. This is penalized unless the horse then clears the obstacle without having to improve its run-up.

The Rules of the Game: Modern Pentathlon

The judges in this competition use points tables for each of the five events. The points system is based on a standard performance earning one thousand points for each sport. The winner is the pentathlete who has accumulated the most points after the five events have been completed.

Shooting (pentathlon)
In the shooting event, the athletes use air pistols to fire twenty shots at a target placed ten metres away. Ten points are awarded for a bulls-eye. Targets are changed for each shot and a score of

Chapter Eight: Modern Pentathlon to Softball

172 out of a possible 200 is worth a thousand points. Every target point above or below 172 is worth plus or minus twelve points respectively.

Fencing (pentathlon)
Épée swords are used in the fencing segment and every competitor must try for one touch against each of the other athletes in the competition. Each bout lasts for one minute. If a hit is not scored within the allotted time, both competitors register a defeat. The target area is the whole body. A total score of seventy per cent victories equals a thousand points with the value of each hit worth twenty-eight points. Fencers are punished for dangerous play and if a person turns his back on another, he receives a ten point penalty.

Swimming (pentathlon)
In the 200m freestyle swimming event, the time of two minutes and thirty seconds gains a male athlete a thousand points. Women can gain the thousand points if they achieve times of two minutes and forty seconds. Every tenth of a second above or below the stated times decreases or increases the points total by one point respectively. Two false starts, or failing to touch the end of the pool while turning, will result in a forty point penalty.

Horse Riding (pentathlon)
The riding segment is a show-jumping contest. It requires a competitor to jump against twelve obstacles. The horse is selected in a draw, twenty minutes before the beginning of the competition. A competitor starts with twelve hundred points and thirty points are lost if an obstacle is knocked down. Forty points are lost by a refusal; sixty points are lost for falling off the horse and three points per second are lost if the time limit is exceeded. If the horse or rider falls twice, then the athlete is disqualified. If a horse refuses the same jump three times, then the rider must move

Chapter Eight: Modern Pentathlon to Softball

on to the next obstacle. A handicapping system is used in the cross-country segment, with the runner's starting point based on his or her total score earned in the first four events.

Running (pentathlon)
In this 3km cross-country segment, runners start running at intervals, as determined by their total scores earned in the first four events. A male athlete who finishes the course in ten minutes earns a thousand points. For women, 11 minutes and 20 seconds earns them a thousand points. Every half-second above or below this standard will lose or gain two points respectively.

Gold medal winners in the Modern Pentathlon, 1988-
Winning athletes' names and countries are given for individual events. The countries they represented are listed for team events.

	Individual	**Team**
Seoul: 1988	Janos Martinek (Hungary)	Hungary
Barcelona: 1992	Arkadlusz Skrzypaszek (Poland)	Poland
Atlanta: 1996	Alexander Parygin (Kazakhastan)	*No competition.*
	Men (Individual)	**Women (Individual)**
Sydney: 2000	Dimitry Svatkovsky (Russia)	Stephanie Cook (Great Britain)
Athens: 2004	Moiseev Andrey (Russia)	Zuzanna Voros (Hungary)
Beijing: 2008	....	....
London: 2012	....	....

Chapter Eight: Modern Pentathlon to Softball

Rowing

Rowing was first used as a means of transport in ancient Egypt, Greece and Rome. It probably became a sport in Victorian England in the 17th and early 18th centuries. Rowing was admitted to the Olympic programme in 1896, but the rough seas in the Piraeus harbour forced the rowing events to be cancelled at these first modern Olympic Games.

Rowing has been changed more often than any other Olympic sport. Categories have been frequently added, modified and discontinued since the event was held successfully in Paris in 1900.

In Athens in 2004, the men's events in this category of sports comprised single sculls, double sculls, quadruple sculls, pair-oared shell without coxswain, four-oared shell without coxswain, eight-oared shell with coxswain, lightweight double sculls and lightweight four-oared shell without coxswain.

Women have been rowing in the Games since 1976. The women's events have comprised single sculls, double sculls, quadruple sculls, pair-oared shell without coxswain, eight-oared shell with coxswain and lightweight double sculls.

The present Olympic programme includes fourteen events. In Athens, in 2004, there were eight men's events and six women's events. The men's events comprised single sculls, double sculls, lightweight double sculls, quadruple sculls, coxless pairs, coxless fours, lightweight coxless fours and coxed eights. Women competed in similar events with the exception of coxless fours and lightweight coxless fours.

Useful Terms: Rowing

Catch a crab	An oar is trapped under water or misses the water when a rower attempts a stroke.
Coxless	Without someone to steer the boat.
Coxwain (cox)	A person who steers a boat.

Chapter Eight: Modern Pentathlon to Softball

Double sculls	A race rowed by two rowers, each using a pair of oars.
Quadruple	With four people in a crew.
Scull	A race between boats with single pairs of oars.
Shell	A light boat used for racing.
Sweep rowing	A type of boat racing in which each rower works with only one oar.

The Rules of the Game: Rowing

In the rowing events, unlike canoeing/kayaking, athletes face backwards during a race. There are two different types of rowing, scull rowing (each rower uses two oars) and sweep rowing (each rower uses only one oar).

The shaft of a sweep oar is between 3.66m and 3.97m long, while that of a scull oar is around three metres long. The blade of a sweep oar is bigger than that of a scull oar.

Rowing is an endurance test with finishes at a speed of up to 10m per second. Crews can cover the middle kilometre of a two kilometre race at about forty strokes per minute but, over the first and last 500m, may shift up a gear to as many as forty-seven strokes per minute The key to winning a race is the ability to synchronise these strokes as perfectly as possible. If one crew member loses rhythm, it is possible that the race will be lost.

In the sweep rowing events, the second rower is in an important position. The first rower is in what is called the "stroke" seat. He sets the pace for the others to follow. But if the second rower, whose oar is on the other side of the boat, does not match the stroke, then rowers on his side will not be synchronizing with the other rowers and the consequence will be that the boat will slow down.

In races that include a coxswain, the coxswain is the only person facing forward and navigates the whole team. He will also call the stroke to synchronise the rowers' rhythm and keep an eye

Chapter Eight: Modern Pentathlon to Softball

on opponents' boats. The weight of the coxswain is regulated. A man must weigh at least 55kg and a woman 50kg. In lightweight events, men should weigh no more than 72.5kg and women no more than 59kg.

Competitions begin with qualifying tests, with the quickest qualifiers moving up to the semi-finals. The top semi-finalists advance immediately to the final. Those rowers who remain participate in a second round for a second chance to reach the semi-finals.

Gold medal winners in Rowing, 1988-
Winning athletes' names and countries are given for individual events. The countries they represented are listed for team events.

SEOUL 1988
Men
Thomas Lange (East Germany)	Single Sculls
The Netherlands	Double Sculls
Great Britain	Coxless Pairs
Italy	Coxed Pairs
Italy	Coxless Quadruple Sculls
East Germany	Coxless Fours
East Germany	Coxed Fours
West Germany	Coxed Eights

Women
Jutta Behrendt (East Germany)	Single Sculls
East Germany	Double Sculls
Romania	Coxless Pairs
East Germany	Coxed Quadruple Sculls
East Germany	Coxed Fours
East Germany	Coxed Eights

Chapter Eight: Modern Pentathlon to Softball

BARCELONA: 1992
Men
Thomas Lange (Germany)	Single Sculls
Australia	Double Sculls
Great Britain	Coxless Pairs
Great Britain	Coxed Pairs
Germany	Coxless Quadruple Sculls
Australia	Coxless Fours
Romania	Coxed Fours
Canada	Coxed Eights

Women
Elisabeta Lipa (Romania)	Single Sculls
Germany	Double Sculls
Canada	Coxless Pairs
Germany	Coxless Quadruple Sculls
Canada	Coxless Fours
Canada	Coxed Eights

ATLANTA: 1996
Men
Xeno Mueller (Switzerland)	Single Sculls
Italy	Double Sculls
Great Britain	Coxless Pairs
Germany	Quadruple Sculls
Australia	Coxless Fours
Netherlands	Eights
Switzerland	Lightweight Double Sculls
Denmark	Lightweight Coxless Fours

Women
Yekatarina Khodotovich (Belarus)	Single Sculls
Canada	Double Sculls
Australia	Coxless Pairs
Germany	Quadruple Sculls

Chapter Eight: Modern Pentathlon to Softball

Romania	Eights
Romania	Lightweight Double Sculls

SYDNEY: 2000
Men

Rob Waddell (New Zealand)	Single Sculls
Slovenia	Double Sculls
France	Coxless Pairs
Italy	Quadruple Sculls
Great Britain	Coxless Fours
Great Britain	Eights
Poland	Lightweight double sculls
France	Lightweight coxless fours

Women

Ekaterina Karsten (Belarus)	Single Sculls
Germany	Double Sculls
Romania	Coxless Pairs
Germany	Quadruple Sculls
Romania	Eights
Romania	Lightweight Double Sculls

ATHENS 2004
Men

Tufte Olaf (Norway)	Single Sculls
Australia	Men's Pairs
France	Double Sculls
Germany	Men's Fours
Poland	Lightweight Double Sculls
Denmark	Lightweight Fours
Russia	Men's Quadruple Sculls
USA	Men's Eights

Women

Rutschow Stomporowski Katrin (Germany)	Single sculls

Chapter Eight: Modern Pentathlon to Softball

Romania	Women's Pairs
New Zealand	Double Sculls
Romania	Lightweight Double Sculls
Germany	Women's Quadruple Sculls
Romania	Women's Eights

Sailing (Yachting)
Sailing was known originally as "yachting" (from the Dutch word, "yaghten", meaning "to hunt"). The word "yachting" was officially changed to "sailing" for the 2000 Olympics. The types of yacht used have changed since sailing was first included in the Olympic competition in 1920. The emphasis is now on the sailing skills of the sailors rather than on the possible maximum speeds of the boats. Boats that required crews of up to ten persons have given way to vessels that are crewed by one person.

Until the 1988 Games in South Korea, sailing events were open to both men and women together but, for the first time, an event was held in that year for women only. Alison Jolly and Lynne Jewell won in the 470 class in the inaugural women-only competition. The 1992 and subsequent Games featured women sailing all of the following: Europe, 470 class dinghies, a new three-person keelboat and Mistral windsurfers. The women's Mistral race in 1996 was won by Lee Lai-shan, the first Hong Kong athlete awarded a gold medal in any Olympic sport.

There are four different types of boats: Mistral, dinghy, keelboat and catamaran. The Mistral is a type of windsurfer consisting of a board with a mast and a sail. Dinghies are small boats manned by one or two persons. Keelboats have keels fixed below their hulls. A catamaran has two hulls with a centreboard and a rudder on each hull, a two-sail rig and a mainsail.

In 2004, the competition was open to the Mistral One Design 2004 Tuned Edition of a Windsurfer; the Finn class; the 470, the Men's Laser and the Star.

Chapter Eight: Modern Pentathlon to Softball

Useful Terms: Sailing

Boom	A horizontal pole securing the bottom of a boat's sail.
Dinghy	Craft with a single sail or two sails and steered by a rudder. Some dinghies have an additional sail called a spinnaker.
Europe	A type of dinghy (used in women's events only in the Olympics).
Finn	A type of dinghy (used only in men's events in the Olympics).
Gaff	A "spar" on a mast that supports the head of a sail.
Gybe	To cause a sail to move; to change course.
Halyard	A rope used for lowering or raising a sail.
Jib	A triangular sail.
Laser	A type of dinghy.
Luff	The edge of a sail next to the mast.
Mistral	A board with a mast and a sail, a type of "windsurfer".
Rudder	A flat piece of wood or steel hinged vertically to a ship for steering.
Soling and Star	These are types of keel boats. They have "fins" below the hull (keel). In addition, the Soling has a spinnaker.
Spar	A strong pole used for the mast of a ship.
Tack	The movement of a boat in zig-zag fashion.
Trapeze	A sliding support used by crew-members for balancing when on a yacht.
49-er	A type of dinghy.
470	Another type of dinghy.
Tornado	A type of catamaran. A catamaran is a boat with twin hulls and a rudder on each hull. This is an open event in the Olympics.

Chapter Eight: Modern Pentathlon to Softball

The Rules of the Game: Sailing

There are two types of racing, match racing and fleet racing. In match racing, competitors race boat against boat. Each competitor tries to manœuvre the other into making mistakes or committing violations. These match races are held on much shorter courses than fleet races.

Fleet racing runs on the principle that the first boat to cross the line wins the race. In all fleet events, there is a series of eleven races, except those featuring the 49er racing dinghy that has sixteen races.

The system of scoring has varied over the years but, at the 2004 Athens Olympics, each boat was awarded minus points depending upon its place in a race. Thus the boat in first place gained one point. The boat that came second gained two points, and so on. At the conclusion of the final race, each boat was allowed to drop its single worst score, except for boats in the 49er class. The winner was the boat with the lowest accumulated score at the end of the race series.

During a race, there are rules governing how boats can move in relation to others. For example, when two boats on opposite tacks meet, the port-tack boat needs to stay clear of the starboard-tack boat. And when two boats on the same tack overlap, the boat closest to the wind must stay clear. Port is the left-hand side (looking forward) of a boat. A tack is the direction in which a boat moves according to the position of its sails. For example, if a boat moves to the right, then it is said to be on a starboard tack.

A sailor who feels that he has been treated unfairly may protest to the judges within ninety minutes of the end of a race. Five judges hear the protest, with other competitors appearing as witnesses for either side.

There are sixteen races for the 49-er class and ten races for the Soling class, followed by a match race competition. A points

Chapter Eight: Modern Pentathlon to Softball

system allocates one point per place, that is, the yacht that comes in first earns one point, the second place, two points, etc. A yacht is considered to have finished a race when its crew, equipment or any part of its hull crosses the finish line.

Gold medal winners in Yachting, 1988-
Winning athletes' names and countries are given for individual events. The countries they represented are listed for team events.

SEOUL: 1988
José Luis Doreste (Spain) — Finn Class
Great Britain — International Star
Denmark — Flying Dutchman
France — International Tornado
USA — 470. Women
France — 470. Men
East Germany — International Soling
Bruce Kendall (New Zealand) — Surfing

BARCELONA: 1992
José van der Ploeg (Spain) — Finn Class
USA — International Star
Spain — Flying Dutchman
France — International Tornado
Spain — 470. Men
Spain — 470. Women
Denmark — International Soling
Franck David (France) — Lechner A-390 Men
Barbara Kendall (New Zealand) — Lechner A-390 Women
Linda Andersen (Norway) — Europe Class

ATLANTA: 1996
Men
Mateusz Kusnierewicz (Poland) — Finn Class

Chapter Eight: Modern Pentathlon to Softball

Ukraine	470
Nikolas Kaklamanakis (Greece)	Mistral Sailboard
Women	
Kristine Roug (Denmark)	Europe
Spain	470
Lee Lai-Shan (Hong Kong)	Mistral Sailboard
Open	
Brazil	Star
Spain	Tornado
Germany	Soling
Robert Scheidt (Brazil)	Laser

SYDNEY: 2000
Men

Iain Percy (Great Britain)	Finn Class
Australia	470
Christoph Sieber (Austria)	Mistral Sailboard
Women	
Shirley Robertson (Great Britain)	Europe
Australia	470
Alessandra Sensini (Italy)	Mistral Sailboard
Open	
USA	Star
Austria	Tornado
Denmark	Soling
Ben Ainslie (Great Britain)	Laser
Finland	49-er

ATHENS: 2004
Men

Ben Ainslie (Great Britain)	Finn Class
USA	470
Robert Scheidt (Brazil)	Laser

Chapter Eight: Modern Pentathlon to Softball

Gal Fridman (Israel)	Mistral
Brazil	Star
Women	
Merrett Faustine (France)	Mistral
Spain	Women's 49er
Norway	Women's Europe
Great Britain	Women's Yngling
Greece	Women's 470
Austria	Women's Tornado

Shooting

The first references to guns as weapons of war were made in the early fourteenth century but shooting as a sport does not seem to have developed until the fifteenth century. Over the years, shooting at wild animals and birds has been recognised as a sport but only once in Olympic history were pigeons used as moving targets in shooting events. Today, competitors shoot at non-animal targets, either still or moving.

The management of worldwide shooting for sport is in the hands of the International Shooting Sport Federation that oversees the World Shooting Championships and co-operates with the Olympic authorities.

Shooting was first included in the Olympic programme in 1896. Recent Olympic competitions for men, for example in the year 2000, have featured air pistol, small-bore rifle (prone), small-bore rifle three positions, air rifle, trap, double trap and skeet in the overall programme. The first Olympic shooting events for women were held in 1984.

Useful Terms: Shooting

Bore	The interior diameter of a gun barrel.
Calibre	A unit of measurement for the bore of a rifle or pistol.

Chapter Eight: Modern Pentathlon to Softball

Firing line — A line where shooting competitors position themselves to shoot at their targets.
Gauge — A unit of measurement for the bore of a shotgun.
Shotgun — A smooth-bore firearm that fires round shots.
Skeet — A target made of clay. This is thrown from a "trap" and imitates the flight of a bird. Targets are released from different heights that are called "low" and "high" houses.
Trap — This releases objects for shooting practice.

The Rules of the Game: Shooting

The types of weapon and the rules for different events have been modified from time to time since the first Olympic "free pistol" competition took place in Athens in 1896. Scoring is done by observing the positions of bullets on the targets. In a final round, the eight leading scorers stand on the firing line together to shoot against each other. Their final round scores are added to their scores in the preliminary round, to find the winner.

Men
Small-Bore Rifle: Prone (lying on the front with the face down). The competitor shoots at a distance of 50m and is given one hour and fifteen minutes for his sixty shots. He is also allowed to use fifteen sighting shots. The diameter of his target, the bulls-eye, is 10.4cm.

Small-Bore Rifle: Three Positions:
The competitor in this event must use a .22 rifle and take forty shots prone, forty shots standing and forty shots kneeling. The target is at a distance of 50m.

Chapter Eight: Modern Pentathlon to Softball

Rapid Fire Pistol
The competitor has eight seconds to fire his .22 calibre pistol at each of five targets. When the targets reappear, he has six seconds to fire and then he must shoot at each of the targets within a four second period. He must repeat the sequence four times.

Pistol
The competitor can take two hours over his sixty shots at a fifty metre target. The bulls-eye is two inches in diameter.

Air Pistol
After a preliminary round, the leading eight competitors participate in a ten-shot final. Seventy-five seconds is allowed for each shot at a target of 11.5M.

Air Rifle
The competitors take sixty shots at a distance of ten metres. There is a time limit of one hour and forty-five minutes.

Trap
This is familiar on cruise ships. The competitor is allowed two shots at each clay bird with a .12-gauge shotgun. The finalists shoot at twenty-five targets.

Skeet
This is similar to trap shooting but the competitor must hold the rifle at his hip until the (clay) target is released into the air.

Running Target
The competitor must use a .177 calibre air rifle to shoot at a target 10m away. The target moves sideways on a two metre rail. There are two rounds. The first round is at a slow speed when the target moves across the rail in five seconds. The second round consists of rapid shooting when the target moves in 2.5 seconds. Each

Chapter Eight: Modern Pentathlon to Softball

competitor fires thirty shots at the target in each round. Telescopic sights are allowed.

Double Trap
The competitors shoot at clay targets from each of five places. The targets (made of clay) are released two at a time. There are one hundred and fifty targets in the preliminary round and fifty targets in the final round.

Women
Sport Pistol
The competitors fire at a distance of twenty-five metres. In the qualifying round, the competitors engage in both precision and rapid fire. The bulls-eye is 5cm across. Ten rapid fire shots test each of the competitors in the final.

Air Pistol
Competitors take forty shots from a distance of ten metres at a bulls-eye of 11.5m in diameter.

Small-Bore Rifle (three positions):
This is the same as the men's competition, except that there are twenty instead of forty shots at each position.

Air Rifle
The women have forty-five minutes in which to fire forty shots at a target that is at a distance of ten metres. The finalists have five more shots and must observe a time limit of seventy-five seconds for each shot.

Trap
The competitors are allowed two shots at each "bird". The top six performers move up to the final where they shoot at twenty-five targets.

Chapter Eight: Modern Pentathlon to Softball

Double Trap
The competitors fire at clay targets from each of five places.

Skeet
There is a seventy-five-shot preliminary round and the competitors with the six highest scores proceed to the final at which twenty-five shots must be fired.

Gold medal winners in Shooting, 1988-

SEOUL: 1988
Men

Miroslav Varga (Czechoslovakia)	Small-Bore Rifle (Prone).
Malcolm Cooper (Great Britain)	Small Bore Rifle (three positions).
Afnasi Kuzmin (Soviet Union)	Rapid Fire Pistol
Sorin Babii (Romania)	Free Pistol (50m)
Tor Heiestad (Norway)	Running Game Target
Taniou Kiriakov (Bulgaria)	Air Pistol
Axel Wegner (East Germany)	Skeet Shooting
Dmitri Monakov (Soviet Union)	Trap Shooting
Goran Maksimovic (Yugoslavia)	Air Rifle

Women

Nino Salukvadze (Soviet Union)	Sports Pistol
Silvia Sperber (West Germany)	Small Bore Rifle (three positions)
Irina Chilova (Soviet Union)	Air Rifle
Jasna Sekaric (Yugoslavia)	Air Pistol

Chapter Eight: Modern Pentathlon to Softball

BARCELONA: 1992
Men

Lee Eun-Chul (Korea)	Small Bore Rifle (prone)
Grachia Penkian (Unified Team)	Small Bore Rifle (three positions)
Ralf Schumann (Germany)	Rapid-Fire Pistol
Konstantin Lukashik (Unified Team)	Free Pistol (50m)
Michael Jakosits (Germany)	Running Game Target
Wang Yifu (China)	Air Pistol
Petr Hrdlicka (Czechoslovakia)	Trap Shooting
Yuri Fedkin (Unified Team)	Air Rifle

Women

Marina Logvinenko (Unified Team)	Sport Pistol (three positions)
Launi Meili (USA)	Small Bore Rifle
Yeo Kab-Soon (Korea)	Air Rifle
Marina Logvinenko (Unified Team)	Air Pistol
Shan Zhang (China)	Mixed

ATLANTA: 1996
Men

Christian Klees (Germany)	Small Bore Rifle Prone
Jean-Pierre Amat (France)	Small Bore Rifle (three positions)
Ralf Schumann (Germany)	Rapid-Fire Pistol
Boris Kokorev (Russia)	Free Pistol (50m)
Ling Yang (China)	Running Game Target
Roberto Di Donna (Italy)	Air Pistol
Ennio Falco (Italy)	Skeet Shooting
Michael Diamond (Australia)	Trap Shooting
Russell Mark (Australia)	Double Trap Shooting

Chapter Eight: Modern Pentathlon to Softball

Artem Khadzhibekov (Russia)	Air Rifle
Women	
Li Duihong (China)	Sports Pistol
Alexandra Ivosev (Yugoslavia)	Small Bore Rifle (three positions)
Renata Mauer (Poland)	Air Rifle
Olga Klochneva (Russia)	Air Pistol
Kim Rhode (USA)	Double Trap Shooting

SYDNEY: 2000

Men	
Jonas Edman (Sweden)	Small Bore Rifle (prone)
Rajmond Debevec (Slovakia)	Small Bore Rifle (three positions)
Serguei Alifirenko (Russia)	Rapid Fire Pistol
Tanyu Kiriakov (Bulgaria)	Free Pistol
Ling Yang (China)	Running Game Target
Franck Dumoulin (France)	Air Pistol
Yalin Cai (China)	Air Rifle
Mykola Milchev (Ukraine)	Skeet Shooting
Michael Diamond (Australia)	Trap Shooting
Richard Faulds (Great Britain)	Double Trap Shooting
Women	
Maria Grozdeva (Bulgaria)	Sport Pistol
Renata Mauer-Rozanska (Poland)	Small Bore Rifle (three positions)
Nancy Johnson (USA)	Air Rifle
Luna Tao (China)	Air Pistol
Zemfira Meftakhetdinova (Azerbaijan)	Skeet Shooting
Daina Gudzineviciute (Lithuania)	Trap Shooting

Chapter Eight: Modern Pentathlon to Softball

ATHENS: 2004
Men

Wang Yifu (China)	Air Pistol
Alipov Alexei (Russia)	Trap Shooting
Zhu Qinan (China)	Air Rifle
Nestruev Mikhail (Russia)	Pistol (50m)
Almaktoun, Ahmed (United Arab Republic)	Double Trap
Emmors Matthew (USA)	Rifle (prone 50m)
Schumann Ralf (Germany)	Rapid Fire Pistol
Benelli Andrea (Italy)	Skeet
Jia Zhanbo (China)	50m Rifle (three positions)
Kurzer Manfred (Germany)	10m Running Target

Women

Du Li (China)	10m Air Rifle
Kostevich Olena (Ukraine)	10m Air Pistol
Balogh Suzanna (Australia)	Trap
Grozdeva Maria (Bulgaria)	25m Pistol
Rhode Kimberley (USA)	Double Trap
Galkina Lioubov (Russia)	50m Rifle (three positions)
Igali Diana (Hungary)	Skeet

Softball

It has been claimed that the modern game of softball originated in Chicago on Thanksgiving Day in 1887. Excited by the news that Yale had beaten Harvard in their traditional annual football (American) match, a group of male supporters invented an indoor game, using an old boxing glove as a ball and a broom handle as a bat. Subsequently, one of the men, named George Hancock, created a better ball and a rubber-tipped bat; drew up some preliminary rules and gave the new activity the name of indoor baseball.

In 1895, a women's softball team was formed in Chicago. Although the women's game developed only slowly, it gradually

Chapter Eight: Modern Pentathlon to Softball

caught on. In a national tournament held in Chicago in 1933, it was accepted equally with the men's game. Today, softball is one of the most popular sports in the United States, played by both men and women competitively, as well as socially.

Softball for women has been included in the Summer Olympic programme since the 1996 Atlanta Games. At present, this women's game seems to be a monopoly of the United States which won gold medals at the 1996 Games, the 2000 Sydney Games and the 2004 Athens' Games.

There are many similarities between baseball (mainly played by men) and softball (most usually played by women). But there are also some important differences. Some of these relate to the pitch and to the "bases". For example, the pitcher's "mound" in softball is level with the ground and at a shorter distance from the "home plate" than it is for baseball. Other differences relate to the equipment used by the players, the weight and circumference of the ball and the length of play. Unlike baseball, the pitcher throws underarm and the match takes place over seven innings instead of nine.

The governing body for softball is the International Softball Federation that holds world championships every four years. There are also several World Cups and, of course, the Olympic Games, open to women's teams since the Atlanta Games in 1996.

As with most of the Olympic events, the softball competition begins with a preliminary round involving eight national teams, made up of the nation hosting the Olympics, three winners from regional tournaments and four semi-finalists from the recent world championships. After the preliminary contests, the top four teams move up to the semi-finals. The best semi-final winner advances straight to the final but the rest need to compete among themselves again. The winner proceeds to the final.

Chapter Eight: Modern Pentathlon to Softball

Useful Terms: Softball

Fast pitch	The pitcher delivers the ball at maximum speed in a flat, smooth arc, making the ball difficult to hit.
Diamond	A pitch or field with a grass surface.
Modified pitch	A kind of pitching in which the pitcher delivers the ball at different speeds.
Pitching Mound	As in baseball, the place from which the pitcher throws the ball.
Slow pitch	A kind of pitching in which the pitcher delivers the ball at a slow speed to deceive the batter.

The Rules of the Game: Softball

The playing field for softball is divided into foul territory and fair territory. Fair territory, in turn, is divided further into an infield and an outfield. Home plate is made of rubber and is five-sided, occupying one corner of a diamond with bases at each corner. These bases are made of canvas and are usually fixed in position. They are numbered anticlockwise as first base, second base and third base.

To score in softball, it is necessary to touch all three of the bases and then home plate. Softball may be played at fast pitch, slow pitch and modified pitch. At fast pitch, the pitcher delivers the ball at maximum speed, making it difficult for the batter to hit it. Slow pitch softball gives the batter more opportunity to hit the ball. Modified pitch places no restrictions on the speed of pitching.

A softball is lighter than a baseball with a circumference of between 28cm and 30.5cm. Despite its name, a softball is as hard as a baseball. Pitchers throw the ball over-arm in baseball but in softball, pitchers are allowed to throw under-arm.

Chapter Eight: Modern Pentathlon to Softball

In baseball a match lasts for nine innings. A softball game is shorter, lasting only for seven innings. In each inning in softball, each team bats until three batters have been declared out.

All batters must wear protective helmets, some with cages that protect the batter's face. The batter is out if three strikes are called, or when a ball hit by the batter is caught before it touches the ground, or the batter is touched by the ball while away from a base.

As with most of the Olympic classes, the softball competition begins with a preliminary round. The top four teams then move up to the finals. Each game ends after seven innings.

Gold medal winning teams for Softball, 1988-

Atlanta: 1996	Sydney: 2000	Athens: 2004
USA	USA	USA
Beijing: 2008	London: 2012	: 2016
....	....	....

The game seems to be a monopoly of the United States where it is played regularly.

Some Key Words and Phrases
Modern pentathlon

Bullseye	Handicapping	Pistol shooting
Discus	Javelin	Points Tables
Rowing		
Coxless	Oar	Sculls
Coxswain	Quadruple	Shell
Sailing		
Catamaran	Mainsail	Rudder
Dinghy	Mistral	Starboard-tack
Hull	Port-tack	Wind-surfer
Keelboat	Rig	Yachting

Forward to Beijing! A Guide to the Summer Olympics

Chapter Eight: Modern Pentathlon to Softball

Shooting
Barrel	Prone	Skeet
Diameter	Rapid fire	Small-Bore
Double-trap	Rifle	Target
Pigeons	Running target	Trap

Softball
Cages	Foul territory	Overarm
Circumference	Helmet	Rubber-tipped
Fair territory	Monopoly	Underarm

QUIZ (modern pentathlon, rowing, sailing, shooting, softball)
1. How many activities are there in a modern pentathlon?
2. In a modern pentathlon, what does a standard performance earn?
3. When was rowing first included in the Olympic programme?
4. What is a, "shell"?
5. When was the Yachting event renamed the Sailing event?
6. When is a yacht considered to have finished a race in the fleet events?
7. What is "skeet" shooting?
8. What are the targets made of in "trap" shooting?
9. Name one important difference between softball and baseball.
10. Which events do the following pictograms indicate?

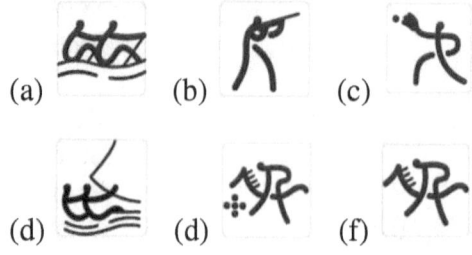

154   Forward to Beijing! A Guide to the Summer Olympics

Chapter Nine

TABLE-TENNIS TO WRESTLING

Table Tennis

Otherwise known as "ping pong", table tennis played a public role in improving diplomatic relations between China and the United States. In 1971, a United States table tennis team visited Japan to participate in a competition. They were then invited to visit China. This invitation came only after a long period of diplomatic negotiations between the two countries.

Accepting the invitation, a small group of American players left for mainland China on 10 April 1971. During their stay, the team played exhibitions and enjoyed themselves as tourists. On 9 July 1971, the then United States Secretary of State, Henry Kissinger, paid a secret visit to China to pave the way for a visit by the then President of the United States, Richard Nixon. This presidential visit took place in February 1972 when Mr Nixon engaged in fruitful discussions with the then Chairman, Mao Zedong and the then Premier, Zhou Enlai.

Table tennis was originally developed to enable tennis players to practice during bad weather. "Ping Pong" was only one of the names given to the game in its early days. Other extraordinary names were "whiff whaff" and "flim flam". Derived from the noise that the ball makes when it is struck by the bat, the name "Ping-Pong" was used more often.

Table Tennis was added to the Olympic programme in 1988.

Useful Terms: Table Tennis

End line	A white line along each end of the playing surface.
Expedite	To conclude a match after a number of

Chapter Nine: Table Tennis to Wrestling

	long rallies by applying a limit to the number of strokes for each point.
Penholder Grip	Holding the bat like a pencil. Sometimes known as the Eastern Grip.
Ping Pong	Table Tennis. The name originates from the sound of a bat striking a ball.
Toss	To throw.
Twiddling	Holding the bat beneath the surface of the table to disguise the type of spin.
Western Grip	Holding the bat with the fingers on the face of the bat.

The Rules of the Game: Table Tennis

New rules were introduced for table tennis in 2004, requiring players to take it in turns to hit two serves at a time, rather than the five serves required in previous competitions. The first of the two players to score eleven points is declared to have won the game. If the score reaches 10-10, then the service must change after each serve, instead of after two serves. The player who wins four games wins the match.

Players must allow a ball played towards them only one bounce on their side of the table and must return it so that it bounces on the opponent's or opponents' side. If the ball doesn't land there, it is counted as a dead ball.

In the Olympics, a single elimination format is followed. In the singles matches, sixteen top seeded players advance to a main draw while forty-eight others contest a qualification round. A second group of sixteen players advances from that round. Winners in the semi-finals play for the gold and silver medals while the losers play for the bronze medal. A similar format is used for all thirty-two teams that are involved. The official rules for Olympic table tennis state that the competitors must wear socks at all times!

Chapter Nine: Table-Tennis to Wrestling

Gold medal winners for Table Tennis, 1988-

SEOUL: 1988
Men
Yoo Nam Kyu (Korea): Singles.
Chen Longcan and Wei Qingguang (China): Doubles.
Women
Chen Jing (China): Singles.
Hyun Jung-hwa and Yang Young-ja (South Korea): Doubles.

BARCELONA: 1992
Men
Jan-Ove Waldner (Sweden): Singles.
Lu Lin and Wang Tao (China): Doubles.
Women
Deng Yaping (China): Singles.
Deng Yaping and Qiao Hong (China): Doubles.

ATLANTA: 1996
Men
Liu Guoliang (China): Singles.
Kong Linghui and Liu Guoliang (China): Doubles.
Women
Deng Yaping (China): Singles.
Deng Yaping and Qiao Hong (China): Doubles.

SYDNEY: 2000
Men
Kong Linghui (China): Singles.
Wang Liqin and Yan Sen (China): Doubles.
Women
Wang Nan (China): Singles.
Li Ju and Wang Nan (China): Doubles.

Chapter Nine: Table Tennis to Wrestling

ATHENS: 2004
Men
Ryu Seung Min (Korea): Singles.
Chen Qi and Ma Ling (China): Doubles.
Women
Zhang Yining (China): Singles.
Wang Nan and Zhang Yining (China): Doubles.

Taekwondo
Taekwondo is a fighting sport, originating in Korea but assuming different names over many centuries. "Tae" means "to kick", "Kwon" means "to punch with the fist or hand" and "Do" means "a method" or "a way."

Although Taekwondo is a very physical sport, it encourages its practitioners to accept that there is a unity of body and mind and that the two should not be separated. Taekwondo is therefore regarded by its teachers and their students as a means of developing character and as a philosophy in its own right. This philosophy is reinforced by a code of conduct based on eleven precepts. They are: an unbeatable spirit, faithfulness to one's spouse, respect for one's brother and sisters, respect for one's teachers, respect for one's parents, respect for one's elders, respect for life that must never be taken unjustly, loyalty to one's country, loyalty to one's friends, loyalty to one's school and finishing what one has begun.

Taekwondo has been claimed to develop strength, balance and flexibility. To achieve these, the student must participate in different aerobic and anaerobic exercises, learn falling techniques and spar with an opponent. Similar to Judo, there are different Taekwondo ranks and, over time, the dedicated practitioner will endeavour to move upwards from one rank to the next.

In 1908, the World Taekwondo Federation was admitted to the International Olympic Committee and at the 1988 and 1992 Olympic Games, taekwondo was designated an official

Chapter Nine: Table-Tennis to Wrestling

demonstration sport. It was added to the Olympic programme at the Sydney Games in 2000. Not surprisingly, both male and female Korean athletes achieved considerable success, taking home three gold medals and a silver medal.

Useful Terms: Taekwondo

Attention area	The area between the boundary of the mat and the combat zone.
Boundary lines	The unmarked marginal lines around the outside of the contest area, defining the outer edge of the mat.
Combat zone	An 8m x 8m area where the main action of a taekwondo contest take place.
Do	The art.
Kwon	Destroy with the fist.
Scoring areas	The areas of the opponent's face or body where a legitimate strike may be made to score a point.
Tae	Foot.

The Rules of the Game: Taekwondo

Sixteen male athletes compete in each weight division. Fifteen female athletes do the same. An opponent can be attacked on the head, the abdomen and the sides of the body by use of the feet below the ankle and the knuckles of the middle and index fingers. The fighters wear body protectors marked with the areas that may be hit. Areas that may not be hit without penalty are the face and the back.

There are four weight categories in Olympic taekwondo: Flyweight, Featherweight, Welterweight and Heavyweight. The scoring areas on a fighter's body are the abdomen, the left and right sides of the body and the head. Points are gained by striking

Chapter Nine: Table Tennis to Wrestling

these specific areas. Points can be deducted if penalties are incurred. There are full-point penalties (for example, attacking the opponent's face) and half-point penalties (for example, for holding or pushing). In the case of a tie, the competitor who scores the most points (after deducting penalties), is the winner.

Gold medal winners in Taekwondo, 1988-

SYDNEY: 2000
Men
Michail Mouroutsis (Greece): 58kg
Steven Lopez (USA): 68kg
Angel Matos Fuentes (Cuba): 80kg
Kim Kyong-hun (Korea): 80+kg
Women
Lauren Burns (Australia): 49kg
Jung Jae-eun (Korea): 57kg
Lee Sun-hee (Korea: 67kg
Chen Zhong (China): 67+kg

ATHENS: 2004
Men
Mu Yen Chu (Taiwan): 55kg
Hadi Sael Bonehkohal (Iran): 68kg
Steven Lopez (USA): 80kg
Dae Sung Moon (Korea): 80kg+
Women
Shih Hsin Chen (China): 49kg
Ji Won Jang (South Korea): 57kg
Wei Luo (China): 67kg
Zhong Chen (China): 67kg+kg

Chapter Nine: Table-Tennis to Wrestling

Tennis

Tennis is known to have been a popular sport in European monasteries in the eleventh century. As time passed, it became a favourite game of kings. At first, the game was played with bare or gloved hands. Today, players use rackets made of technically advanced materials.

Tennis was one of the modern Olympics' original sports, introduced in 1896. It featured in all the Games held up to and including those organized in Paris in 1924, after which it was dropped from the programme. There followed a long gap until the game was brought back at Seoul in 1988.

As is the case with football (soccer), tennis is very well known to the general public because of constant and intensive television coverage.

Useful Terms: Tennis

Advantage	The next point won after deuce.
Baseline	The end boundary at either end of a tennis court.
Deuce	The score of "40 all" (i.e. forty to each side) at which two consecutive points are needed to win.
Fault	If a ball is hit outside the court (or "box") it is called a "fault".
Let	A service of the ball not in accordance with the rules. The server is entitled to another serve.
Love	This means "zero" in tennis.
Rally	A long exchange between the opposing players.
Serve	To deliver a ball to begin or resume play.
Set	The part of the match completed when one player or team wins at least six games and is

	ahead by at least two games, or has won a tie-breaker.
Service court	The area of the court where a served ball must land.
Tie-breaker	The deciding game in a set in which the first player or team to score seven points, with a two-point lead, wins the set. This is played when the score is tied at six games all.

The Rules of the Game: Tennis

Tennis is played on a court measuring 23.77m x 8.23m. In doubles matches, the court is extended by 1.37m on both sides. A net of 91.4cm in height divides the court. A baseline is painted at each end of the court and there is a service line drawn 6.4m from the net and parallel to it. Perpendicular to the net, a centre service line is drawn between the sidelines, extending to a service line.

In tennis, a player gains a point if his or her opponent is unable to return the ball within the baseline and the sidelines on his/her opponent's side of the court. Players serve from the baseline from one side of the court to the diagonal service court of the opponent's side. Service alternates between the two halves of the court.

In a tennis game, a zero point or score is called "love" When a player wins a point at the beginning of a match, the score is fifteen. The score for the second point is thirty. A third point leads the score to forty. If the player scores a fourth point, he then wins the game. If both players have reached forty points, then the score is called "deuce". A point scored by a player after deuce is an "advantage" for that player. A following point will lead to victory in the game. However, if the opponent wins the next point, then the score is returned to deuce.

The game must continue until one player wins two clear points after deuce. The first competitor to gain seven points is

Chapter Nine: Table-Tennis to Wrestling

declared the winner of the set. In Olympic tennis, matches are won by the first player to win two sets, except in the men's finals when a "best of three sets out of five" determines the winner.

In the Olympics, players are seeded according to their world ranking. Based on their progress in the annual Wimbledon tournament, the leading forty-eight players in the world are qualified to enter the Olympic tournament. National entries are, however, restricted to three singles players and one doubles team each for both men and women. After seeding, a draw is made. All matches are elimination rounds until the semi-finals. The two semi-final winners play for gold and silver medals; the two semi-final losers compete for the bronze medal.

Gold medal winners for Tennis, 1988-

SEOUL: 1988
Men
Miloslav Mecir (Czechoslovakia): Singles.
Ken Flach and Robert Seguso (USA): Doubles.
Women
Steffi Graf (West Germany): Singles.
Pam Shriver and Zina Garrison (USA): Doubles.

BARCELONA: 1992
Men
Marc Rosset (Switzerland): Singles.
Boris Becker and Michael Stich (Germany): Doubles.
Women
Jennifer Capriati (USA): Singles.
Gigi Fernandez and Mary Jo Fernandez (USA): Doubles.

Chapter Nine: Table Tennis to Wrestling

ATLANTA: 1996
Men
Andre Agassi (USA): Singles.
Mark Woodforde and Todd Woodbridge (Australia): Doubles.
Women
Lindsay Davenport (USA): Singles.
Gigi Fernandez and Mary Jo Fernandez (USA): Doubles.

SYDNEY: 2000
Men
Yevgeny Kafelnikov (Russia): Singles.
Sebastian Lareau and Daniel Nestor (Canada): Doubles.
Women
Venus Williams (USA): Singles.
Venus Williams and Serena Williams (USA): Doubles.

ATHENS: 2004
Men
Massu Nicolas (Chile): Singles.
Massu Nicolas and Gonzalez Fernando (Chile): Doubles.
Women
Henin-Hardenne Justine (Belgium): Singles.
Li Ting and Sun Tian Tian (China): Doubles.

Triathlon
In 1974, the triathlon was introduced at Mission Bay in the handsome city of San Diego as a variation on single track events. A so-called Ironman Triathlon was staged in Hawaii in 1978, requiring competitors to swim 3.86km, cycle 180.2km and run 42.2km. Today, triathlon events are held in different parts of the world. The Olympic distance — a 1.5km swim, a 40km cycle ride and a 10km run — has now become accepted as the standard course or the international distance.

The triathlon may not be the ultimate endurance test —

Chapter Nine: Table-Tennis to Wrestling

perhaps that "honour" should go to the modern pentathlon — but it is difficult enough, requiring the athletes to excel at three very different disciplines. Each contestant competes against the clock and the course. The three triathlon events are usually placed back to back and the scoring includes the time necessary to change from one event to another, including changing caps, wet suits (if worn) and shoes. This adds to the tension felt by the contestants in the event for, not only must they be good swimmers, cyclists and runners but, like actors in a costume play, they must also be skilled at quick changes.

Useful Terms: Triathlon

Bricks	Combined bicycle and run workouts involving repeated intervals of each discipline.
Disciplines	Activities that train people's minds and bodies.
Drafting	In the context of triathlon cycling and swimming, a technique whereby one competitor follows another competitor closely, to benefit from the suction effect.
Transition	The period in between stages of the triathlon where competitors change equipment for the next discipline (for example, from swimming to cycling and from cycling to running).

The Rules of the Game: Triathlon

As the name implies, the Triathlon tests three skills: swimming (1,500m) cycling (40km) and running (10,000m). The times taken to complete each of the three sports are totalled to find the champion.

Chapter Nine: Table Tennis to Wrestling

Swimming (triathlon)
The competition begins with swimming. Contestants dive into the water from a floating platform. All swimming strokes are allowed but, obviously, nearly all the competitors choose the fastest stroke, the crawl. All the competitors are required to wear bathing caps and goggles. If the temperature of the water is below fourteen degrees Celsius, the contestants must wear wet suits. Over certain parts of the course, some advantage may be gained by "drafting".

Cycling (triathlon)
Once the swimming leg is completed, athletes remove their caps, wet suits (if worn) and goggles; put on their helmets and cycling shoes and mount their bicycles. The cycling leg takes place around a pre-marked course and is completed at the point where the race has begun. To keep muscles flexible and loose, special bicycles are used with aero-bar handlebars, aerodynamically-shaped wheels and angled seats. When riders reach the finishing line, they must quickly place their bicycles on a rack and then change into running shoes before they begin on the last phase of their trial.

Running (triathlon)
The triathlon running segment is the most testing part of the competition, largely because the whole body is tired and the muscles ache after the swimming and cycling events. Many athletes find that the transition from cycling to running causes them to run at a slower pace than might have been the case if they had not been obliged to perform in the first two disciplines. Recognising this phenomenon, the athletes train by switching from cycling to running and from running to cycling in workouts called "bricks" (the popular name given to exercises involving two sport disciplines).

    The rules are most strict when dealing with changeovers

Chapter Nine: Table-Tennis to Wrestling

between disciplines. One athlete must not impede another, or interfere with an opponent's equipment. If this happens during the swimming leg, then the offender is made to stop for thirty seconds at the end of the leg before continuing. If violations occur during the cycling leg, the offender will be given a yellow card and must not continue the race until he is given official permission. Two yellow cards lead to a red card and hence disqualification.

At Olympic level, the first event of this kind was held in Sydney in 2000.

Gold medal winners in the Triathlon, 1988-

	Men	**Women**
Sydney: 2000	Simon Whitfield (Canada)	Brigitte McMahon (Switzerland)
Athens: 2004	Hamish Carter (New Zealand)	Kate Allen (Australia)
Beijing: 2008	....	....
London: 2012	....	....

Volleyball

Dr James Naismith is said to have invented basketball in 1891. Not to be outdone, a YMCA physical fitness instructor, W.G. Morgan, developed volleyball in 1895 as a game to be played by middle-aged men; a game that would require less physical contact and that would not be as strenuous as basketball.

Modelled on badminton, the game was originally called Mintonette ("Minton" from the word, "Badminton" and "ette" meaning, "smaller") However, during a game at an American university, one of the spectators noticed that the players were volleying the ball over the net and the consequence was that the sport was renamed "Volleyball". Volleyball became an Olympic sport at the Tokyo Games in 1964.

Chapter Nine: Table Tennis to Wrestling

Useful Terms: Volleyball

Block	To return the ball with the hands by jumping at the net to stop an opponent's smash.
Double contact	A foul when the ball touches a player twice consecutively or rolls along a part of his body.
Floater	An overhand serve when the ball is hit with no spin so that its path becomes unpredictable. This type of serve can be administered while jumping or standing.
Jump serve	An overhand serve when the ball is tossed high in the air, then the player makes a timed approach and jumps to make contact with the ball.
Libero	A substitute defensive player.
Mintonette	The original name for volleyball.
Set	A set is a group of games. A set is won when a team reaches fifteen points for indoor volleyball.

The Rules of the Game: Volleyball

In contrast to basketball, in which the players shoot into a netted basket, the players in volleyball throw, that is, they volley, a large ball over a net. The ball weighs between 260kg and 280kg. The game is played on a court that measures 18m x 9m. This court must be divided in the centre by a net 9.5m long, suspended 2.43m above the floor for men and 2.24m above the floor for women.

The game is played by two opposing teams of six players, with up to six substitutions allowed during breaks in play. One of the six players on each side is named the "libero". He wears a

Chapter Nine: Table-Tennis to Wrestling

different coloured shirt from the rest of the team and plays a purely defensive role. As such, he is forbidden to attack, serve or block.

At the beginning of each point, three players in each team stand near the net and three operate from the back of the court. They may leave their positions after the serve. Players try to knock the ball over the net while stopping the ball from landing on the floor of their court. The same player cannot touch the ball twice consecutively but his team may touch it up to three times in knocking it back to their opponent's half of the court. The ball must pass over the net inside the limits of the side net markers. If the ball touches one of these markers, then a point is lost.

Two referees and four line judges control the game. The first referee validates the points gained and blows his whistle if he observes a foul or a double contact.

A service may be taken from anywhere behind the end line. There are different types of serve, namely a spin serve, a jump service and a "floater". The service goes to the team that has scored the last point. But when a team regains service, a different player must take it.

A match is played over five sets. The first side to score twenty-five points with a two-point advantage wins the set. If a final set is needed, the first side to score fifteen with a two-point advantage wins the match.

Gold medal winning teams for Volleyball, 1988-

	Men	Women
Seoul: 1988	USA	USSR
Barcelona: 1992	Brazil	Cuba
Atlanta: 1996	The Netherlands	Cuba
Sydney: 2000	Yugoslavia	Cuba
Athens: 2004	Brazil	China
Beijing: 2008	....	....
London: 2012	....	....

Chapter Nine: Table Tennis to Wrestling

Weightlifting

Weightlifting is a very ancient activity, practised in China, Greece and Egypt thousands of years ago. Originally, stones and boulders were used as weights but, eventually, these were replaced by "dumb-bells" and metal weights. The word "dumb-bell" is derived from the use of bells in churches and other buildings, with the clappers removed. Today, dumb-bells have been replaced by barbells, that is, bars with discs. In Olympic contests, these weights vary from 0.25kg to 25kg. They are distinguished from each other by colour.

Weightlifting for men was first included in the programme of the 1896 Athens Games but with only two categories, one-armed lifting and two-armed lifting. A British athlete, Launceston Elliot, won the one-armed event with a lift of 71kg. He thought that he had also won the two-armed event but, because he moved his feet during his lift, he was awarded second place to the Danish athlete, Viggo Jensen.

Women's weightlifting was introduced to the Olympic Games in Sydney 2000, with seven weight categories. In the 2004 Athens Games, women competed with China, Russia, Turkey, Bulgaria, Thailand and Ukraine and, among them, shared fifteen medals.

Useful Terms: Weightlifting

Bar	The steel shaft that forms the base of a barbell.
Barbell	A piece of equipment consisting of a steel bar and rubber-coated discs of different weights.
Clean and Jerk	There are two movements. The athlete lifts the bar to the chest in one movement and then above the head in a second movement, with the arms fully stretched.

Chapter Nine: Table-Tennis to Wrestling

Good lift	A successful weightlifting performance.
No lift	An unsuccessful weightlifting performance.
Press	A lift in which an athlete lifts the barbell to his shoulders from a crouched position and then presses it above his head while keeping his back straight.
Snatch	The athlete raises the bar (with weights attached to each end) in one movement without pausing.
Squat	Dropping the barbell while bending the legs.

The Rules of the Game: Weightlifting

Weightlifting, like wrestling, was popular long before the first Olympic tournament. We know that Games were held as early as 708BC. For the Greeks, wrestling was part of everyday life.

The sport of weightlifting has been affected in recent years by drug scandals. Because of this, all weight categories were changed after the 1992 Barcelona Olympics and they were changed again in 1998.

There are general rules covering different types of "lifts". For example, in all lifts the referee must count as "no lift" any unfinished try in which the bar is at the height of the knees. In all lifts, if the bar is stopped before arriving at the shoulders, or arms length, the attempt will be judged, "No lift." In all lifts, touching the platform with any part of the body other than the feet will be judged "No lift."

In the Athens Games in 2004, each athlete was allowed three attempts at each type of lift. Each performed the snatch and the clean and jerk in eight different weight categories for men, and seven different weight categories for women. A competitor who attempted the snatch had to lift the bar above his or her head in one movement and hold it in that position for two seconds. A

Chapter Nine: Table Tennis to Wrestling

competitor who attempted the clean and jerk had to bring the bar up to his or her collarbone or the chest, and then raise the bar overhead so that his or her arms were extended vertically.

Each competitor in the weightlifting category is allowed one minute from the time his or her name is called until he or she begins to lift. To qualify for a total mark, a weightlifter is required to perform successfully one lift in each category.

Weightlifters are allowed to compete in one or more than one group. An individual contestant is allocated to a group after his or her possible performance is estimated. For both the snatch and the clean and jerk, each group's competition is regarded as final. The results of the different groups in one category are combined and a final ranking is then calculated.

Three referees assess each competition and carry out the weigh-in procedures for each contestant.

Gold medal winners in Weightlifting, 1988-

SEOUL: 1988

Sevdalin Marinov (Bulgaria)	Flyweight
Oken Mirzoian (Soviet Union)	Bantamweight
Nahim Suleymanoglu (Turkey)	Featherweight
Joachim Kunz (East Germany)	Lightweight
Borislav Gidikov (Bulgaria)	Middleweight
Israil Arsamakov (Soviet Union)	Light-Heavyweight.
Anatoli Khrapaty (Soviet Union)	Middle-Heavyweight
Pavel Kuznetzov (Soviet Union)	First Heavyweight
Juri Zacharevich (Soviet	Second Heavyweight

Chapter Nine: Table-Tennis to Wrestling

Union)
Alexander Kurlovich (Soviet Union)   Super Heavyweight

BARCELONA: 1992
Ivan Ivanof (Bulgaria)   Flyweight
Chan Byung-Kwan (Korea)   Bantamweight
Naim Suleymanoglu (Turkey)   Featherweight
Israel Militosiyan (Unified Team) Lightweight
Fedor Kassapu (Unified Team)   Middleweight
Pyrros Dimas (Greece)   Light Heavyweight
Kakhi Kakhiashvili (Unified Team) Middle-Heavyweight
Viktor Tregubov (Unified Team)   First Heavyweight
Ronny Weller (Germany)   Second Heavyweight
Alexander Kurlovich (Unified Team) Super Heavyweight

ATLANTA: 1996
Halil Mutlu (Turkey)   Flyweight
Tang Ningsheng (China)   Bantamweight
Naim Suleymanoglu (Turkey)   Featherweight
Zhang Xugang (China)   Lightweight
Pablo Lara (Cuba)   Middleweight
Pyrros Dimas (Greece)   Light-Heavyweight
Alexei Petrov (Russia)   Middle-Heavyweight
Akakidei Khakiashvilis (Georgia) First Heavyweight
Timur Taimassov (Ukraine)   Second Heavyweight

Chapter Nine: Table Tennis to Wrestling

Andrei Chemerkin (Russia)   Super-Heavyweight

SYDNEY: 2000
Women competed in Weightlifting for the first time in the Sydney Olympics.
Men
Halil Mutlu (Turkey)	-56kg
Nikolay Pechalov (Croatia)	56-62kg
Galabin Boevski (Bulgaria)	62-69kg
Xugang Zuan (China)	69-77kg
Pyrros Dimas (Greece)	77-85kg
Akakios Kakiasvilis (Greece)	85-94kg
Hossein Tavakoli (Iran)	94-105kg
Hossein Rezazadeh (Iran)	105+kg

Women
Tara Nott (USA)	-48kg
Xia Yang (China)	48-53kg
Soraya Jimenez Mendivil (Mexico)	53-58kg
Xiaomin Chen (China)	58-63kg
Weining Lin (China)	63-69kg
Maria Isabel Uruttia (Colombia)	69-75kg
Meiyuan Ding (China)	75+kg

ATHENS: 2004
Men
Halil Mutlu (Turkey)	56kg
Zhiyong Shi (China)	62kg
Guozheng Zhang (China)	69kg
Taner Sagir (Turkey)	77kg
George Asanidze (Georgia)	85kg
Milen Dobrev (Bulgaria)	94kg
Dmitry Berestov (Russia)	105kg

Chapter Nine: Table-Tennis to Wrestling

Hossein Reza Zadeh (Iran) 105+kg

Women
Taylan Nurcau (Turkey) 48kg
Udomporu Polsak (Thailand) 53kg
Yangqing Chen (China) 58kg
Natalia Skakun (Ukraine) 63kg
Chunhong Liu (China) 69kg
Pawaina Thongsuk (Thailand) 75kg
Gonghong Tang (China) 75+kg

Wrestling: Freestyle and Greco-Roman

Records show that wrestling was introduced into the ancient Olympics in 708BC, but cave drawings have revealed that wrestling was popular long before the first Games were held. For the Greeks, wrestling was part of everyday life, regarded as a way of achieving symmetry and grace in strenuous activity. Wherever and whenever it was convenient, free-born men in Greek society would gather together to witness and to participate in contests of balance and strength that had only one style.

Sculptures and etchings on coins and vases indicate that the purpose was for one opponent to throw another down so that his hip, shoulders and back would touch the ground. A man who threw his opponent down three times would be regarded as the winner. Although such a fall might be disturbing, it has been said that Greek wrestling was seldom brutal.

Useful Terms: Wrestling

Boston Crab	One wrestler sits on the back of his opponent with legs tucked under his or her arms.
Central wrestling area	The circle on a wrestling mat where the main action of wrestling takes place.

Chapter Nine: Table Tennis to Wrestling

Cross Buttock	A wrestler throws an opponent over his or her hip.
Fall	A situation when an athlete forces his opponent's shoulders to the mat for a touch to halt and win the bout.
Flying Mare	One wrestler throws his or her opponent over his or her back. The opponent's arm is used as a lever.
Irish Whip	A one-handed throw in which the opponent's arm is pulled backwards and forwards, forcing the opponent to somersault in the air.
Mat Chairman	The only chief official who is allowed to communicate with the judge and the referee. He indicates his decisions by raising a wrestler's colour.
Passivity Zone	The outer circle on a wrestling mat.
Pile Driver	The opponent is turned upside down and his head is pushed into the canvas.
Sleeper	Pressing nerves in the neck to cause unconsciousness.
Sudden Death	A way of making a decision in a "tied" game.

The Rules of the Game: Wrestling

Wrestling events today are divided into Freestyle and Greco-Roman wrestling. For both types of wrestling, there are seven weight categories for men and four for women.

Chapter Nine: Table-Tennis to Wrestling

Freestyle Wrestling
Freestyle wrestling matches were held in the 1904 and 1908 Olympic Games but were dropped from the programme until 1924. The rules for freestyle wrestling are quite specific. Contestants begin a bout on a 12m x 12m mat. The central wrestling area is a yellow circle, nine metres in diameter. A one metre red circle is known as the passivity zone. The red circle is there to warn wrestlers that they are near to the edge of the competition area.

The objective of the sport is to bring down an opponent so that he cannot move and his shoulders are pinned to the mat for two seconds. This is known as a "fall" which automatically ends a bout. A victory can also be gained by winning ten points in a bout. This is known as "technical superiority". Points are awarded for successful holds, positions of advantage and near-throws.

Each bout consists of two three-minute rounds, with a thirty-second break in between the rounds. A wrestler who wins two rounds wins the bout. For final victory, a wrestler must gain at least three technical points. If scores are tied, the bout goes into "sudden-death" overtime when the next contestant to score wins. If neither wrestler gains a point by the end of overtime, then the winner is chosen by a majority vote of the judge, the referee and the mat chairman. A win can also be declared when an opponent is injured too badly to continue wrestling or is disqualified because he does not appear when his name is called for a contest.

Greco-Roman Wrestling
Greco-Roman wrestling was invented, neither in Greece nor in Rome, but rather in nineteenth-century France. The name given to this new form of wrestling was chosen to honour the contributions made by both ancient Greece and Rome to the development of the sport.

Greco-Roman wrestling differs from freestyle wrestling in several ways, for example, the wrestler may not hold his opponent

Chapter Nine: Table Tennis to Wrestling

in any part of the body below the hips and he may not use his legs to press, squeeze or push his opponent.

As in the freestyle form of the event, the wrestlers in Greco-Roman wrestling are categorised by weight. A maximum weight limit (of 130kg) was imposed in the Seoul 1988 Olympics. 20 wrestlers in each weight category are divided into six pools. The winners in two four-person pools move straight into a semi-final round. Winners in the remaining four three-person pools enter a quarter-final round. The two quarter-final winners proceed to the semi-finals.

Gold medal winners in Wrestling, 1988-

Greco-Roman Wrestling
SEOUL: 1988
Vincenzo Maenza (Italy)   Light-Flyweight
Jon Rönningen (Norway)   Flyweight
Andras Sike (Hungary)   Bantamweight
Kamandar Madzhidov (Soviet Union)   Featherweight
Levon Zhulfalakian (Soviet Union)   Lightweight
Kim Young Nam (Korea)   Welterweight
Mikhail Mamiashvili (Soviet Union)   Middleweight
Atanas Komchev (Bulgaria)   Light-Heavyweight
Andrzej Wronski (Poland)   Heavyweight
Alexander Karelin (Soviet Union)   Super Heavyweight

BARCELONA: 1992
Oleg Kucherenko (Unified Team)   Light Flyweight
Jon Rönningen (Norway)   Flyweight.
Han Bong An (Korea)   Bantamweight
Akif Pirim (Turkey)   Featherweight
Attila Repka (Hungary)   Lightweight
Minazakan Iskandarian (Unified   Welterweight
Team)

Chapter Nine: Table-Tennis to Wrestling

Peter Farkas (Hungary)	Middleweight
Maik Bullmann (Germany)	Light-Heavyweight
Hector Milian (Cuba)	Heavyweight
Alexander Karelin (Unified Team)	Super-Heavyweight

ATLANTA: 1996
Sim Kwon Ho (Korea)	Light Flyweight
Armen Nazarian (Armenia)	Flyweight
Yovei Melnichenko (Kazakhstan)	Bantamweight
Wlodzimierz Zawadzki (Poland)	Featherweight
Ryzsard Wolny (Poland)	Lightweight
Feliberto Aguilera (Cuba)	Welterweight
Hamza Yerlikaya (Turkey)	Middleweight
Vyachetslav Oleynyk (Ukraine)	Light-Heavyweight
Andreas Wronski (Poland)	Heavyweight
Alexander Karelin (Russia)	Super-Heavyweight

SYDNEY 2000
Kwon-Ho Sim (Korea)	48-54kg
Armen Nazarian (Bulgaria)	54-58kg
Vartares Samourgachev (Russia)	58-63kg
Feliberto Azcuy (Cuba)	63-69kg
Mourat Kardanov (Russia)	69-76kg
Hamza Yerlikaya (Turkey)	76-85kg
Mikael Ljungberg (Sweden)	85-97kg
Rulon Gardner (USA)	97-130kg

Note: Armen Nazarian has represented two different countries: Armenia at Atlanta, Bulgaria (after immigrating there) at Sydney, winning a gold medal at each.

ATHENS: 2004
Majoros Istvan (Hungary)	55kg
Jung Ji Hyun (Korea)	60kg
Mamsurov Farid (Azebadjan)	66kg
Dokturishivili Alexandre (Uzbekistan)	74kg

Chapter Nine: Table Tennis to Wrestling

Michine Alexei (Russia)   84kg
Ibrahim Karam (Egypt)   96kg
Baroev Khasan (Russia)   120kg

Freestyle Wrestling
SEOUL: 1988
Takahi Kobayashi (Japan)   Light Flyweight
Mitsuru Sato (Japan)   Flyweight
Sergei Beloglassov (Soviet Union)   Bantamweight
John Smith (USA)   Featherweight
Arsen Fadzayev (Soviet Union)   Lightweight
Kenneth Monday (USA)   Welterweight
Han Myung Woo (Korea)   Middleweight
Macharbek Hadatchev (Soviet Union) Light-Heavyweight
Vasile Puscasu (Romania)   Heavyweight
David Gobedishvili (Soviet Union)   Super-Heavyweight

BARCELONA: 1992
Kim Il (North Korea)   Light-Flyweight
Li Hak-Son (North Korea)   Flyweight
Alejandro Puerto (Cuba)   Bantamweight
John Smith (USA)   Featherweight
Arsen Fadzayev (Unified Team)   Lightweight
Park Jang-Soon (South Korea)   Welterweight
Kevin Jackson (USA)   Middleweight
Marhabeg Chadartsev (Unified Team) Light-Heavyweight
Leri Chabelov (Unified Team)   Heavyweight
Bruce Baumgartner (USA)   Super-Heavyweight

ATLANTA: 1996
Kim Il (North Korea)   Light Flyweight
Valentin Jordanov (Bulgaria)   Flyweight
Kendall Cross (USA)   Bantamweight
Thomas Brands (USA)   Featherweight

Chapter Nine: Table-Tennis to Wrestling

Vadim Bogiyev (Russia)	Lightweight
Buvaisa Saityev (Russia)	Welterweight
Khadshimurad Magomedov (Russia)	Middleweight
Rasul Khadem Azghadi (Iran)	Light-Heavyweight
Kurt Angle (USA)	Heavyweight
Mahmut Demir (Turkey)	Super Heavyweight

SYDNEY: 2000

Namik Abdullayev (Azerbaijan)	48-54kg
Alireza Dabir (Iran)	54-58kg
Mourad Oumakhanov (Russia)	58-63kg
Daniel Igali (Canada)	63-69kg
Brandon Slay (USA)	69-76kg
Adam Saitiev (Russia)	76-85kg
Saghid Mourtasaliyev (Russia)	85-97kg
David Moussoulbes (Russia)	97-130kg

ATHENS 2004

Men

Batirov Maviet (Russia)	55kg
Quintana Yandro Miguel (Cuba)	60kg
Tedeyev Elbrus (Ukraine)	66kg
Saytiev Buvaysa (Russia)	74kg
Sanderson Cael (USA)	84kg
Gatsalov Khadjimourat (Russia)	96kg
Taymazov Artur (Uzbekistan)	120kg

Women (*included for the first time*)

Merleni Irini (Ukraine)	48kg
Yoshida Saori (Canada)	55kg
Icho Kaori (Japan)	63kg
Wang Xu (China)	72kg

Chapter Nine: Table Tennis to Wrestling

Some Key Words
Table tennis

Diplomacy	Expedite	Spin
Endline	Ping Pong	Toss

Taekwondo

Abdomen	Knuckles	Precepts
Body Protector	Martial art	Punch
Code	Penalty	Weight
Index finger	Philosophy	categories

Tennis

Baseline	Let	Sideline
Deuce	Rally	Tie-break(er)
Fault	Serve	Volley

Triathlon

Back to back	Endurance test	Tension
Bricks	Excel	Transition
Discipline	Quick change	Violation

Volleyball

Attack	Floater	Regain service
Consecutive	Jump service	Service
Court	Libero	Spin serve
Defensive	Net	Volley

Weightlifting

Dumb-bell	Crouched	One-armed
Barbell	position	Two-armed

Wrestling

Balance	Pin to the mat	Symmetry
Grace	Pools	Technical
Mat chairman	Specific	superiority
Passivity zone	Strenuous	Wrestler

Chapter Nine: Table-Tennis to Wrestling

QUIZ (table-tennis, taekwondo, tennis, triathlon, volley-ball, weightlifting, wrestling)

1. When were new Olympic rules introduced for table tennis?
2. When was table tennis added to the Olympic programme?
3. How many points must a player have in order to win a table tennis game?
4. When was tennis restored to the Olympic programme?
5. How many games must a player win in order to win a set in tennis?
6. What does "Tae" mean in the word, Taekwondo?
7. Which areas of the body may not be hit without penalty in Taekwondo?
8. What three skills are tested in the Triathlon?
9. Who is said to have invented volleyball?
10. Name the three types of serve in volleyball.
11. How many weight categories were there for men in the weightlifting competition at the 2004 Olympic Games in Athens?
12. Name two ways in which Greco-Roman Wrestling differs from Freestyle Wrestling.
13. Which events do the following pictograms represent?

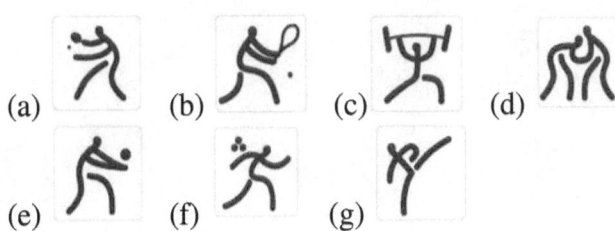

(a)   (b)   (c)   (d)
(e)   (f)   (g)

Forward to Beijing! A Guide to the Summer Olympics   183

KO Lai Chak (L) & LI Ching (R), Hong Kong, China. Men's table-tennis doubles silver medal winners, awards ceremony, Athens Olympics, 2004. *Photo Courtesy SFOCHKC.*

Chapter Ten

CHINA AND THE OLYMPIC GAMES

The Winter Games: A February Frolic
Two hundred and one countries are now recognized by the International Olympic Committee. Taking the 2004 Games in Athens as a guide, it is likely that at least two hundred countries will send teams to compete in the 2008 Summer Games in Beijing. A much smaller number of nations participated in the 2006 Winter Games which took place from 10 to 26 February in the city of Torino, and other sites, in the Italian Alps. The Olympic Village was located in Torino itself. Two stadia in the city — Communale and Della Alpi — were earmarked as the venues for ice hockey, short track, speed skating and figure skating. Other villages in the Alps welcomed athletes competing in such sports as snowboarding, curling, ski jumping, alpine skiing. bobsleigh and the biathlon.

China's record in the Winter Games has gradually improved since its athletes first appeared on winners' platforms at Albertville (France) in 1992. Two silver medals were presented in that year to Ye Qiabo for her performance in the womens' 500m and 1,000m speed skating event. That Ms Ye's feat was no fluke became evident in the 1994 Lillehammer (Norway) Games, at which she won a bronze medal in the 1,000m competition. China's progress continued and the country's athletes performed well in the controversial Salt Lake City (USA) Games of 2002, gaining two gold, one silver and two bronze medals. In 2006 China improved again on its haul of medals, gaining a total of eleven, two of which were gold (Xiaopeng Han and Meng Wang), four were silver and five were bronze.

Germany led the medal "league table" with eleven gold medals and a total of 29 medals, closely followed by the United States with nine gold medals and a total of twenty-five medals.

Chapter Ten: China and the Olympic Games

China's first gold medals
The first athletes representing China to win gold medals did so at the Los Angeles Summer Games in 1984. The first to win was sharpshooter, Xu Haifeng. The first woman among them was Wu Xiaoxuan who won gold in standard small-bore rifle shooting.[16] Speaking in 1993, when Beijing was among the cities bidding to host the 2000 Olympiad, Timothy Fok, now President of the Sports Federation and Olympic Committee of Hong Kong, China and a member of the International Olympic Committee, spoke about these early successes and also about what participation and success in the Olympic Games meant for Chinese people.[17]

A Triumph for Hong Kong
In 1996, a year before Hong Kong was returned to China, the city rejoiced when the windsurfer Lee Lai-shan won the gold medal for wind-surfing at the Atlanta Games. When the news of her victory became known, tens of thousands of Hong Kongers took to the streets to celebrate her success. San San, as she is affectionately known, dedicated her medal to the athletes of Hong Kong. As of 2007, she remains the only Hong Kong athlete who has won an Olympic gold medal.

Summer Successes
China lost its 1993 bid for the year 2000 Summer Games to Sydney by only two votes. There was, therefore, some disappointment in the country when the International Olympic Committee voted to hold the 28th Summer Games in Athens in 2004. It was felt by some that an opportunity to benefit from the experience gained at the 1990 Asian Games in Beijing the 1993 East Asia Games in Shanghai, and the 1996 Asian Winter Games in Harbin had been missed.

Try and Try Again
Undeterred, China submitted a comprehensive application to the

Chapter Ten: China and the Olympic Games

International Olympic Committee to host the 29th Summer Olympic Games in 2008. There was great jubilation when it was announced on Friday, 13 July 2001 that Beijing's final bid against Istanbul, Paris, Osaka and Toronto had been successful. Beijing had gained fifty-six of the one hundred and five votes in the second and last round of voting.

The Environment
China's plan emphasized the need for a "Green Olympics". Symbolically, this has now been achieved by re-naming Olympic Park, "Olympic Green".
 Practical measures are under way to solve Beijing's well-known pollution problems by means of a clean-air campaign and the construction of a new water-treatment system. Steel mills and factories have been relocated and the authorities in Beijing have announced that Beijing will close some factories for a period of three months before the Games take place. New ring roads are under construction and there are to be seven new subway lines, one built to whisk visitors and others from a renovated airport to the downtown area, and the other to take people from downtown to the Olympic Green. One of the new north-south subway lines opened in the Autumn of 2007 and two more lines are scheduled to open in July 2008.
 State of the Art digital and video technical support will be provided for the Games and the Government has declared that priority is to be given to the improvement and protection of the environment in the design and construction of new Olympic facilities and venues.

Culture and Education
Aspects of traditional Chinese culture will not be neglected. To this end, a Department of Cultural Activities was linked to the Beijing Organising Committee for the 2008 Games (BOCOG). At a conference co-organised by the Department and held in Beijing

Chapter Ten: China and the Olympic Games

in 2004, Professor Jin Yuanpu referred to the cultural significance of the logo, "Dancing Beijing", which has been adopted for the 2008 Games. Coloured red, it symbolizes joy, happiness, hope and good luck. According to Professor Yuanpu, this red seal stands for trust and sincerity, whilst the Chinese characters that are engraved upon it reveal "economy in expression, ambiguity and richness in meaning".

The mascots adopted for the games are the five Fuwa (the "Five Friendlies"), a panda, a fish, an antelope, a swallow and the Olympic flame. These correspond to the five elements of Chinese philosophy, Huanhuan, Yingying, Nini, Jingjing and Beibei and represent the five Olympic Rings incorporated in the Olympic Flag. Commenting on an article which appeared in the *Beijing Daily* on 4 November 2007, the *South China Morning Post* noted that more than 4,000 people share their names with one or other of these five mascots. Nearly 3,500 children have been named for the Olympics, most of them born around the year 2000.[18]

In 2005, the Beijing Olympic Committee declared that the slogan, "One World, One Dream", had been adopted for the Games. This decision was made after 210,000 entries had been received in a global search for appropriate words.

On 7 August 2006, the official countdown to the Games was marked by the issue of thirty-five icons, representing Olympic sports. These icons are based on seal character pictograms and are represented in the Quiz sections in this book.

On 8 August 2006, Mr Timothy Fok Tsun Ting lit an Olympic flame in Kowloon Park to indicate that only two years remained before the launch of the Games in Beijing.

New educational programmes, linked to the Games, are being introduced and the government aims to enhance international friendship in many different ways, for example, by fostering people-to-people cultural exchanges. Cultural tourism will be catered for but a plan to protect Beijing's cultural and historical heritage will also be implemented. World heritage sites

Chapter Ten: China and the Olympic Games

such as the Forbidden City and the Great Wall will be placed at the head of the protection list.

The Essential Volunteers
A volunteer programme was launched in June 2005 at a ceremony in Beijing attended by Jacque Rogge, the President of the International Olympic Committee and Liu Qi, the President of the BOCOG. According to the BOCOG, approximately 70,000 volunteers will contribute to the success of the Olympics. They will include many secondary school and college students.

The Venues
Olympic-related construction work is well advanced, following the technical requirements laid down by the International Olympic Committee and the International Sport Federations. Thirty-six of the thirty-seven competition venues were completed by the end of 2007, including the Wukesong Indoor Stadium and the Beijing National Aquatics Centre ("The Ice Cube"). The National Stadium ("The Bird's Nest") is expected to be completed in March 2008. The stadium will seat approximately 80,000 people and will serve as the venue for the opening and closing ceremonies of the Games, as well as the finals of athletics and soccer competitions. Additional venues are still being constructed and existing facilities are being enlarged or improved. Five venues will be made available outside Beijing. New stadia are being erected at Qingdao (International Sailing Centre), Tianjin and Qinhuangdao and the Shenyang Wulihe and Shanghai Stadia are being renovated. Olympic venues have been equipped with special acoustic and photoelectrical aids for disabled competitors.

All the venues will be easily accessible to the public and their post-Games' use has been carefully planned. For example, the building earmarked during the Games for fencing, tennis, wrestling, badminton and the modern pentathlon will be easily convertible into an exhibition and convention centre.

Chapter Ten: China and the Olympic Games

Housing and Medical Services for the Visitors
According to a statement made in May, 2005 by Beijing's vice mayor, the Beijing Organising Committee for the 2008 Games has signed agreements with eighty-eight hotels that will provide 22,962 hotel rooms and thirty-one villas for athletes and other participants. It has also designated twenty hospitals to provide medical services and carry out checks for any use of performance-enhancing drugs.

The Programme for 2008
The final programme for the XXIX Olympics in Beijing has now been agreed. The number of different sports has been capped at twenty-eight, with about 10,500 athletes including 2,069 women expected to take part in different events.

When Is A Sport Not A Sport?
What constitutes a sport? The Oxford English Dictionary defines it as "a game or competitive activity, especially an outdoor one involving physical exertion". This definition does not rule out indoor sports (for example, judo, netball, fencing), neither does it define a sport as necessarily one that requires physical exertion. This lack of a conclusive definition has caused the Olympic Commission some difficulty, since requests to include games such as bridge and chess have been made by their "Recognised Federations". After considerable deliberation, the Commission agreed that "mind sports" are "sports where the physical elements are not necessarily performed by the player in the conduct of the competition" and that such mind sports should not be eligible for admission to the Olympic Programme. This seems to have been a wise decision for, if bridge and chess are allowed, why not poker?

China at the Forefront
China came to the forefront in international Olympic competition after its athletes won fifteen gold medals at the Summer Games

Chapter Ten: China and the Olympic Games

held in Los Angeles in 1984. The number plummeted at the Summer Games held in Seoul in 1988 (five gold medals) but there was a significant recovery in 1992 in Barcelona (sixteen gold medals); in Atlanta in 1996 (sixteen gold medals); in Sydney in 2000 (twenty-eight gold medals), and in Athens in 2004 where China, with a total of thirty-two gold medals, came second only to the United States in the overall competition.

These striking improvements have sprung first from the athletes' fierce desire to excel. They also reflect a degree of commercial sponsorship and years of systematic planning by government agencies, in particular, the centralized China Sports Bureau.

Training for the Olympics begins at an early age. The parents of children with potential are encouraged to enroll them in a government-funded sports school. There are approximately three thousand of these schools situated all over China. About one hundred of these are boarding schools that offer both academic and physical education. The school in Shanghai that trained Liu Xiang is a good example. Liu earned a gold medal in the 110m final in Athens and is now famous all over China. Liu's coach, Sun Haiping, felt that Liu might reach the top six but was hesitant to forecast the gold medal victory that was achieved.

In the nation's capital, the Shishahai sports school can be proud of its record as a training and educational institution. Five of their former students were successful at the Athens Games. Four of these won gold medals. The fifth returned with a bronze medal.

At the Beijing Games in 2008, competing athletes from the participating countries will live in the Olympic "Village". China's athletes have the opportunity to adjust themselves to this situation at the State Sports General Administration's National Training Centre. They train at the Centre throughout the year for their different disciplines. This is where the national teams develop further their expertise in track and field events,

Chapter Ten: China and the Olympic Games

weightlifting, volley-ball, swimming, diving and badminton.

The Eighth of August
The eighth of August 2007 was a significant day in China. It was marked by many thousands of people who gathered together in Beijing's Tiananmen Square to usher in the Games that are scheduled to begin on 8 August 2008 at 8.08pm. The number eight is regarded as especially lucky in Chinese culture.

Exceeding the Goal
China's stated goal at the Athens Games was twenty gold medals. This goal was exceeded handsomely, with thirty-two gold, seventeen silver and fourteen bronze medals as the final total. China's gold medal winners at Athens have attracted national attention and a surge of pride in their achievements.

Gold medal winners of the People's Republic of China at the Athens Games

Athletics
Xiang Liu (Men's 110m hurdles). Equalled the World Record.
Huina Xing (Women's 10,000m).
Badminton
Zhang Ning (Women's Singles).
Zhang Jiewen/Yang Wei (Women's Doubles).
Zhang Jun/Gao Ling (Mixed Doubles)
Canoeing
People's Republic of China (Guanliang Meng/Wenjun Wang) (C2 500m) Canoe Doubles.
Diving: Men
Jia Hu (10m Platform)
Bo Peng (3m Springboard).
People's Republic of China (Liang Tian/Jinghui Yang) (Synchronised 10m Platform)

Chapter Ten: China and the Olympic Games

Diving: Women
Jingjing Guo (3m Springboard)
People's Republic of China (Minxia Wu/Jingjing Guo) (Synchronised 3m Springboard)
People's Republic of China (Lishi Lao/Ting Li) (Synchronised 10m platform)
Gymnastics
Haibin Teng (Men's Pommel Horse)
Judo
Dongmei Xian (Women's Half Lightweight)
Shooting
Zhanbo Jia (50m Rifle 3 Positions)
Qinan Zhu (10m Air Rifle: 60 shots)
Yifu Wang (10m Air Pistol: 60 shots)
Li Du (Women's 10m Air Rifle: 40 shots)
Swimming
Xuejuan Luo (100m Breaststroke)
Table Tennis
Qi Chen/Lin Ma (Men's Doubles)
Yining Zhang (Women's Singles)
Wang Nan/Zhang Yining (Women's Doubles)
Taekwondo
Wei Luo (57-67kg)
Zhong Chen (Over 67kg)
Tennis
Li Ting / Sun Tian Tian (Women's Doubles)
Volleyball
People's Republic of China (Women)
Weightlifting
Zhiyong Shi (Men's 56-62kg) *An Olympic Record.*
Guozheng Zhang (Men's 62-69kg)
Yanging Chen (Women's 53-58kg) *An Olympic Record.*
Chunhong Liu (Women's 63-69kg) *A World Record.*
Gonghong Tang (Women's Over 75kg) *A World Record.*

Chapter Ten: China and the Olympic Games

Wrestling
Xu Wang (Women's 63-72kg)

From this list, it can be seen that, up to late 2007, China's particular strengths (three or more gold medals) are in Badminton, Men's and Women's Diving, Shooting, Taekwondo and Weightlifting.

Some Key Words

Accessible	Excel	Mind (-games)
Bid	Fluke	Pentathlon
Comprehensive	Host	Ring (roads)
Controversial	Jubilation	Seal
Culture	League Table	Stadium / Stadia
Dedicate	Logo	Venue
Earmarked	Mascots	Whisk

QUIZ
1. How many countries are now recognized by the International Olympic Committee?
2. When did China first begin to win at the Winter Olympic Games?
3. By how many votes did China lose its 1993 bid for the 2000 Summer Olympic Games?
4. What did China's plan for the 2008 Olympics envisage?
5. What is the name of the building that will be regarded as the centrepiece of the 2008 Games?
6. How many different sports will be included in the 2008 Games?
7. Approximately, how many sports schools are there in China?
8. Where was Liu Xiang trained?
9. What was China's goal at the Athens Olympics?

Chapter Eleven

THE OLYMPICS IN THE HONG KONG MEDIA

A countdown to the Beijing Olympics began in Tiananmen Square in September 2004. An enormous clock began to count the days, hours and minutes before the Games are to begin. A similar clock has been erected in Qingdao in Shandong Province where the sailing events will take place. Hong Kong, the host for the equestrian events, has not been left out. Passengers hurrying to catch their MTR (Mass Transit Railway) trains at the City's Central Station can hardly miss a colourful display that reveals the number of days left before the opening ceremony on 8 August 2008.

On New Year's Eve 2007, Hong Kong's Radio and Television Hong Kong (RTHK) Company began an Olympic countdown in partnership with China Beijing TV whilst, in January, a new series, *Glamour of Sport,* highlighted the many preparations being made for the successful administration of the Olympics. It is heartening to know that efforts are being made to provide digital TV services so that we can all enjoy clearer pictures of the different events.

Competitors in nine of the twenty-eight Olympic sports could, if they were so inclined, boast that they will be participating in games that have been on the programme since the Olympics were revived in 1896. Aquatics, Athletics, Cycling, Fencing, Gymnastics, Shooting, Tennis, Weightlifting and Wrestling are still on the list although they vary in popularity, at least as measured by TV ratings. If it was necessary to find "Angels" (financial backers) to support TV coverage for these sports, Aquatics, Athletics, Cycling, Fencing, Gymnastics, Shooting and Tennis would do well. Supporters of Rowing and Weightlifting would need to exercise extra powers of persuasion.

Hong Kong people's interest in the Games has increased

Chapter Eleven: The Olympics in the Hong Kong Media

substantially since the countdowns began and stories on many different subjects have appeared in the local media. Some of these stories have been sad, for example, the report that a young member of China's shooting squad had been shot dead by accident during a practice session. Some have been optimistic, for example, the forecast that the Beijing Olympics will make a profit of US$20 million to US$30 million despite the increased budget of US$2.4 billion. Some have been ludicrous, for example, the news that one of the Games' future vegetable suppliers had been fertilizing his plants with milk. (Now if it had been brandy....)

The saying "practice makes perfect," can be applied to many of the activities that have taken place since China's bid to hold the Olympic Games proved successful. One such activity was the Good Luck Beijing Hong Kong Special Administrative Region (HKSAR) 10th Anniversary Celebration Invitation Cup Evening Competition held in Hong Kong from 11 to 13 August 2007. The International Olympic Committee President, Jacques Rogge, found time to visit the Beas River Cross Country Course and later met with the Acting Chief Executive, government officials and Hong Kong sportspersons.

The Hong Kong "Good Luck" Competition was one of twelve that took place at different Olympic venues throughout China. Three such competitions were held at the Shun Yi Rowing and Canoeing Park (Rowing and Canoe/Kayaking), two at the Olympic Green hockey and archery fields and one each at the Qingdao Olympic Sailing Centre, the Chaoyang Park Beach Volleyball ground, the Laoshan Bicycle (BMX) venue, the Road Cycling course and the China Agricultural University Gymnasium. Whilst worthwhile in themselves, these competitions provided invaluable opportunities to rehearse systems and procedures for the international events to come.

Language and other Notes for Visitors & Hosts

Language One

Communicate! Survive in English in Beijing!

You have arrived in Beijing to attend the 29th Olympiad. You have found somewhere to stay; bought a map; and seen some of the venues. You are waiting eagerly for the first games to begin. Visitors in your lodgings or hotel may need to use English to communicate their wishes and thoughts. Like you, they may be strangers to Beijing and they may ask you to help them.

But first, you may wish to ask yourself these questions:
- Can I use courtesy words such as "excuse me" and "thank you?"
- Can I greet people and part from them correctly?
- Can I ask basic questions such as "who", "what", "when" and "where?"
- Can I begin and end a conversation in a polite manner?
- Can I introduce myself or someone else?
- Can I give simple directions to visitors?
- Can I thank visitors and make simple requests?
- Can I answer questions about my nationality, occupation, marital status, age and place of birth?
- Can I deal with simple business at a post office, a pharmacy, a supermarket or a bank?
- Can I talk about my favourite sport or athlete?
- Can I talk about things that might happen in the future or that might have happened in the past?
- Can I describe my work?
- Can I talk about topics of general interest, such as current events and the weather?

Language & other Notes for Olympic Visitors & Hosts

Conversations
The following typical conversations relate to the Summer Games. They provide reminders of how to do the following in English:

- Greet people
- Make introductions.
- Request and deny a name.
- Ask the way and give directions.
- Ask and say where people are.
- Give instructions and make requests.
- Agree and disagree politely.
- Express preferences.
- Make offers and respond to offers.
- Congratulate someone.
- Apologise.

Greet people
Alice Li: Good afternoon, Sir. Welcome to Beijing! What's your name, please?
Mr Biondi: My name's Matt.
Alice Li What's your family name, please?
Mr Biondi: It's Biondi.
Alice Li: Thank you, Mr Biondi.

Make introductions
Ian Thorpe: Aaron, May I introduce Robert Archer? Robert, this is Aaron Peirsol. Aaron won gold medals for the 100metre backstroke and 200metre backstroke in the Athens' Games.
Robert: How do you do? I'm very pleased to meet you, Mr Peirsol.
Aaron: How do you do? I'm pleased to meet you, too, Mr Archer. Welcome to the Games!

Request and deny a name
Receptionist: Good morning, Sir. Is your name Marco?

Language & other Notes for Olympic Visitors & Hosts

Simon Fairweather: No, it isn't. It's Fairweather.
Receptionist: Ah, yes, Mr Fairweather. You're here for the Games, Sir.
Simon Fairweather: Yes, that's right. I've come to watch the archery competition.
Receptionist: Welcome to Beijing, Sir. I know that you are a famous archer.
Simon Fairweather: Thank you. That's very kind of you.

Ask the way and give directions: 1
Veronica Campbell: Excuse me. Can you tell me the way to the Exhibition Centre?
Woman: Yes, certainly. You are now in Baishiqiao Lu. Walk to the end of the street. Turn left into Xizhhimen Dajie. The Exhibition Centre is on the left, past the Zoo.
Veronica Campbell: Thank you very much.
Woman: Not at all.

Ask the way and give directions: 2
Kelly Holmes: Good morning! Can you tell me the way to the National Olympic Stadium?
Man: I beg your pardon. I'm sorry, I don't know. I'm a stranger in Beijing. I'm from Guangzhou.
Kelly Holmes: Oh — what shall I do?
Man: Please ask an Olympic Guide.
Kelly Holmes: Thank you, I will.
Kelly Holmes (*to a Guide*): Excuse me, can you tell me the way to the National Olympic Stadium?
Olympic Guide: What events, Madam?
Kelly Holmes: Athletics.
Olympic Guide: The Stadium's behind those trees, Madam.
Kelly Holmes: Can you show me the way?
Olympic Guide: Yes, certainly. Please follow me.
Kelly Holmes: Thank you very much.

Language & other Notes for Olympic Visitors & Hosts

Ask and say where people are
Mr Taufik Hidayat: Mr Zhu, good morning.
Mr Zhu: Good morning, Mr Hidayat. How are you?
Mr Hidayat: I'm fine, thanks. How are you?
Mr Zhu: Very well, thank you, Mr Hidayat.
Mr Hidayat: Mr Zhu. Is Mr Yang here this morning?
Mr Zhu: No, Mr Hidayat, he isn't. He's gone to a meeting at the NOSC.
Mr Hidayat? The NOSC?
Mr Zhu: Yes — the National Olympic Sports Centre. Mr Yang is a member of the ITF.
Mr Hidayat: ITF?
Mr Zhu: Yes — the International Tennis Federation.
Mr Hidayat. Thank you, Mr Zhu. My game's Badminton.
Mr Zhu: Yes, I know. You won a gold medal in the singles at Athens.
Mr Hidayat: Yes, that's right. Thank you.
Mr Zhu: Not at all, Mr Hidayat. May I wish you a happy time in Beijing!
Mr Hidayat: That's very kind of you. Thank you very much.

Give instructions and make requests
Kelly Holmes: Good afternoon. Could you please tell me the name of this street?
Mr Lin: Good afternoon. Yes – this is Jianguomenwai Dajie.
Kelly Holmes: Ah, good! My hotel is in this street.
Mr Lin: Excuse me. Aren't you Kelly Holmes, the famous runner?
Kelly Holmes: Yes, I am Kelly Holmes. But am I famous?
Mr Lin: You won two gold medals in the Athens Games.
Kelly Holmes: Yes, I did. You have a good memory.
Mr Lin: A wonderful performance! Now — what is the name of your hotel, Ms. Holmes?
Kelly Holmes: The Gloria Plaza. But I don't want to go to the hotel. I want to go to the Friendship Store. Can you help me,

please? I've been looking for it for quite a long time.
Mr Lin: Yes, of course. I'll take you there, Ms. Holmes.
Kelly Holmes: Oh, will you? You are most kind.
Mr Lin: Not at all. It's a pleasure.

Agree and disagree politely
Man: The athletics' competition follows the IAAF Rules.
Woman: IAAF?
Man: International Amateur Athletics Federation.
Woman: Ah, yes. If there is a disagreement over the Rules, "the French version will prevail".
Man: I'm sorry. I don't agree. The English version will prevail.
Woman: The English version?
Man: Yes, the Rules written in English. Of course, other events have their own Rules. For example, the Fencing event has FIE Rules.
Woman: FIE?
Man: Federation Internationale d'Escrime. And in the Rules for Fencing, "the French version will prevail!"

Express preferences
David Lam: Hello, Mr Hoy. How are you?
Chris Hoy: I'm fine, thanks, Mr Lam. How are you?
David Lam: Fine, thank you. Mr Hoy, do you like the Shooting and Taikowondo events?
Chris Hoy. Yes, I do, but I prefer cycling.
David Lam: So do I, Mr Hoy. I prefer cycling too.
Chris Hoy: Is this your first Olympiad?
David Lam: No, I went to the Olympics in Sydney. I watched the cycling there and Mr Hoy, I watched you in Athens. You won a gold medal in the one kilometre time trial.
Chris Hoy. Yes, I did. It's nice of you to remember.
David Lam: I shall never forget. It was very exciting.

Language & other Notes for Olympic Visitors & Hosts

Make offers and respond to offers
Edward: I'm Edward White. Can I offer you some coffee or tea?
Reporter: No, thanks. Can I talk to you about the Olympics, Mr White?
Edward: Yes, certainly. My wife is a gymnast.
Reporter: Yes, I know, Mr White. May I tell you about our bid for the Games?
Edward: Yes, I did read about it. But please remind me. I'm very interested.
Reporter: We received fifty-six votes, but we only needed fifty-two votes to win.
Edward: Yes, I know. May I make some notes?
Reporter: I'm the reporter, Mr White! But please make some notes.
Edward: Why did China win?
Reporter: We have one-fifth of the world's population. Our market for business is very big. We have good venues, including state-of-the art facilities for gymnasts.
Edward: My wife will be pleased. Of course, you have very good athletes. In Athens you earned more medals than any other country, except the United States.
Reporter: Yes, that's correct. Now, Mr White, tell me more about yourself.
Edward. Very well. I was born . . . .

Congratulate someone
Coach: I'd like to be the first to congratulate you. You did very well indeed.
Runner: I tried hard today but I want to do very much better in the semi-final.
Coach: I'm sure you will, but your performance was excellent today. Congratulations again on a splendid effort.
Runner: Thank you, coach, for your kind words, but we both know that I need to run faster for a medal.

Language & other Notes for Olympic Visitors & Hosts

Coach: You will, I am sure. There'll be a medal and a record!
Runner: I'll certainly do my best, with your help.
Coach: Right! We'll go for a gold!

Apologise
Bob (*Shouting*): You were late for the team meeting.
Mary: I know. I'm awfully sorry. I forgot my bag.
Bob: But you were late. It was an important meeting. You knew that. Why didn't you telephone?
Mary: Pardon?
Bob: I said why didn't you telephone?
Mary: Oh – I'm sorry. I tried to telephone but you didn't answer.
Bob: You should support the team. They support you.
Mary: I don't know what to say. I'm really terribly sorry. I hope you will forgive me.
Bob: Mary, I must apologise for shouting at you. But don't be late again.
Mary: I won't. I promise.

TELEPHONING

There are different forms of telephone language:

Introducing ourselves
Hello, this is Zhao Shensheng. Can I help you?

Identifying ourselves
Huo Yongzhe: Could I please speak to Cheng Keqing?
Cheng Keqing : Speaking, or "Cheng Keqing speaking".

Asking for a number
Could I have 63012266 please? That's the Bei Wei Hotel.
Hello. Could I have 64612412, please? Extension 124.

Language & other Notes for Olympic Visitors & Hosts

Apologising
I'm afraid you've got the wrong number.
Is that the number of your mobile? No, it isn't.

Making a request
Can you send me a text message, please? I'm an Olympic Volunteer.

Talking to the operator
Is that the operator? It's not? Sorry, I thought I did dial zero!
I need to make an overseas call to Boston, USA.
I think that the area code is 617, but can you please check?
It is? Thank you, Operator.
I'm sorry, Operator. The line is very bad. Please try again.
Do I have to pay for local calls? I do? What is the rate for each local call? How many minutes do I get for that? Do I still have to pay if no-one answers? I do! I see!
Can I make a call after midnight?
Hello, can you help me to have a morning wake up call? ... Yes, I can see the instructions to set the automatic alarm myself, but I am worried that I will not do it correctly. I really do need to wake up at the right time. Can you please do it from your machine?
Good evening, Operator. I don't want any phone calls now. I'm going to sleep now. Please can you ask all callers to leave a message? I'll call them back in the morning. Thank you.

Talking to room service
Good evening? Room Service? I would like to order something from the room service menu, please. Club sandwich with brown bread, toasted. Does it come with French fries? It does? Good. How long will it take? I'm very hungry. Fifteen minutes? That's fine! Thank you!

Language & other Notes for Olympic Visitors & Hosts

Language Two

Common words and expressions to help you to communicate successfully in English before, during and after the Beijing Olympics

NOTE: In some cases, both short forms and long forms (e.g. "is not/ isn't") are listed below, as alternatives.

Please
Thank you very much
Yes/No
You're/ You are welcome
I'm/ I am sorry
I beg your pardon
Good morning
Good afternoon
Good evening
Good night
Goodbye

Do you understand?
Yes, I understand.
I'm/ I am sorry. I don't/ do not understand.

I speak a little English.
Do you speak Chinese/ Cantonese/ Putonghua?

How do you say…in English?

Excuse me, could you please repeat that?

My name is…
What's/ What is your name?

Language & other Notes for Olympic Visitors & Hosts

How are you?
Very well, thank you.

I'm/ I am lost.// We're/ We are lost.// They're/ They are lost.
Which way did they go?
They went to the right.
They went to the left.
They went straight ahead.
They went that way.
They went the other way.
They went round the corner.

How much is it?
How much does it cost?
It's/ It is very expensive.

I'm/ I am thirsty.
I'm/ I am hungry.
I'm/ I am tired.

Wait!
Listen!

I've/ I have lost my…

Hurry up, please!
Be careful, Sir/Madam!

Money
You can change your money at the bank.
There is a bank in the Olympic Town.

Accommodation
The volunteer will take you to your hotel.
We've/ We have given you a double room with bath.

Language & other Notes for Olympic Visitors & Hosts

There's/ There is a TV set in the room.
You can use your computer in your room.
All our rooms are air-conditioned.
Can I see your passport, please?
Here's/ Here is your key card. Just put it into the slot on the door and then withdraw the card.

Transport
You can take the subway.
There's/ There is a taxi stand over there.
The buses run every ten minutes.

Photography
There's/ There is a camera shop in the Sports Centre.
You can buy films in the Sports Centre.
They sell digital cameras in the Sports Centre.

Souvenirs
There's/ There is a gift shop in the Olympic Town and there are many other fine shops in Beijing.

Personal Care
There's/ There is a beauty salon (parlour) near your hotel.
There's/ There is a barber in the Olympic Town.

Health
There's/ There is a doctor's clinic in your hotel.
There's/ There is a pharmacy in the Olympic Town.

Communications
There's/ There is a Post Office in the Olympic Town.
There's/ There is a fax machine/copier in your hotel.
You can send e-mails from your room.
You can use your mobile phone in Beijing.

Language & other Notes for Olympic Visitors & Hosts

Clothing
You don't need to wear a tie.
Remember to wear comfortable shoes.
The hotel laundry is very good.
Be sure to wear a hat when you go out. The sun's/ The sun is very strong.
Long trousers are more suitable than shorts.

Food
The coffee shop's/ The coffee shop is on the third floor.
In Hong Kong, some excellent Chinese snacks are called "Dim Sum". Do they have them in Beijing too?
The restaurant serves very good tofu (bean curd). It also has excellent Yunnan ham and wonderful mushrooms.
You can get a western breakfast in your hotel. But you may like to try a Chinese breakfast, rice soup ("congee") and a long deep-fried doughnut stick.
There's/ There is a restaurant in the National Stadium ("The Bird's Nest").

Shopping
In many small shops you can bargain.
There are very good shops in your hotel.
The Friendship Store will pack and dispatch your purchases to your home address, or anywhere that you want.
Most large shops will accept credit cards.

Changing money
You can change money at the airport but you can also change it at your hotel front desk. The rates of exchange may be different at the two places.

Language & other Notes for Olympic Visitors & Hosts

Language Three

Questions Visitors may ask and suggested answers from Volunteer Helpers at the Beijing Olympics

Q. Where is /Where's the toilet/ lavatory/ washroom/ bathroom?
A: It's at the end of the passage on the left.

Q: Where is the restaurant?
A: It's on the third floor.
A: It's at the end of this street, on the left.

Q: Where's the dining-room?
A: It's on the second floor.

Q: Where's the office?
A: It's on the fifteenth floor.
A: It's in that building over there.

Q: Where's the entrance?
A: It's round the corner.

Q: Where's the exit?
A: It's at the end of the passage.
A: It's there, on the right.

Q: Where's the taxi stand?
A: It's over there.
A: It's on the other side of the street.

Q: Where's the telephone?
A: It's over there.
A: It's in the office.
A: It's on my desk.

Language & other Notes for Olympic Visitors & Hosts

Q: Can I use my cell phone here?
A: Yes, you can. (*OR* Sorry, no.)

Q: Where's the copier?
A: It's in the office, near the water cooler.

Q: Where's the railway station?
A: You go down this street and turn left at the intersection. It's on the right-hand side.
A: It's behind the Post Office.

Q: When will the bus come?
A: At five o'clock.

Q: When will the plane leave?
A: At fourteen hundred hours.

Q: When does the fencing start?
A: At 10 o'clock.

Q: How much is the fare?
A: It's twenty renminbi.

Q: How much are the souvenirs?
A: Ten renminbi each.

Q: Who is the manager?
A: His name is Mr Weng.

Q: Who is the driver?
A: Mr Tse.

Q: Why are they late?
A: Because the bus broke down.

Language & other Notes for Olympic Visitors & Hosts

Q: Why are the gates closed?
A: Because it's too early.

Q: Why are we waiting?
A: Because it isn't time yet.

Q: How can we go there?
A: By train.
A: By bus.

Q: What is the time?
A: It's ten o'clock.

Q: Is there an internet café anywhere?
A: If you want to use the internet, you can try the business centre at your hotel.

Q: I'm allergic to peanuts. How can I be sure that the food doesn't have peanuts in it?
A: You can ask the waiter.
Q: Suppose he doesn't know?
A: Then ask him to ask someone who does know!

Q: Are there any licensing laws? Can we drink an alcoholic drink at any time?
A: As long as a bar or restaurant is open, and serves alcoholic drinks, you can order one there.

Q: What about smoking? Are there strict laws about smoking?
A: If you're not allowed to smoke anywhere, there will be a notice saying so. Don't worry about it.

Language & other Notes for Olympic Visitors & Hosts

Language Four

The Hong Kong Visitors

Talking to Mr van Grunsven

Visitor	Excuse me, Sir. Can you help me? I'm from Thailand and I plan to come to watch the Olympics in Hong Kong.
Van Grunsven	I'll do my best. What can I do for you? You are aware, of course, that only the equestrian events will be held in Hong Kong.
Visitor	Yes, I know. I'm sorry to trouble you but I think that I've seen your picture in the newspaper. Are you Mr van Grunsven?
Van Grunsven	Yes, that's correct.
Visitor	You won the individual jumping competition in Athens.
Van Grunsven	And the individual dressage competition.
Visitor	Yes, of course. I remember now.
Van Grunsven	How can I help you?
Visitor	Well, I understand that the dressage and show-jumping competitions will take place in Shatin. Can you tell me how to get there? Is it a big city?
Van Grunsven	No. Shatin is not really a city but it's quite a large town. You're now in Queen's Road Central on Hong Kong Island. Shatin is in the New Territories. One quick way to get there is to take the "MTR" – the mass transit railway – to Mongkok. Then change platforms and take the MTR again to the Kowloon Tong station and then, finally, take a third train to Shatin. When you get to Shatin, you can take a taxi to

Language & other Notes for Olympic Visitors & Hosts

	the Hong Kong Sports Institute where the Olympic Competitions will be held.
Visitor	Thank you. That's extremely helpful.
Van Grunsven	Not at all. I hope you enjoy the competitions.
Visitor	I'm sure I shall. It was a pleasure to talk to you, Mr Grunsven.

Equestrianism

Visiting Student	What does equestrianism mean?
Visiting Teacher	It means the skill of horsemanship.
Student	Did I pronounce it correctly?
Teacher	Yes, you did; but it's not easy. Too many consonants.
Student	There's another funny word to do with the Olympics.
Teacher	Yes?
Student	I mean, "Dressage".
Teacher	You pronounced that correctly too. Good. It's a French word taken from the French verb, "*dresser*", meaning "to train". The horse is trained to perform special movements under the direction of the rider.
Student	But what is, "horsemanship"?
Teacher	It means knowing about horses.
Student	I understand. But I still have a lot to learn about equestrianism.

Many ways to travel

Visitor	I understand that there are over six million people in Hong Kong.
Hong Kong Resident	Yes, we are a bit crowded.
Visitor	How do all these people get from "A" to "B"?

Language & other Notes for Olympic Visitors & Hosts

Resident   I don't like to boast but I think that it's true to say that we have one of the best transport systems in the world.
Visitor   You have buses and trains, of course.
Resident   Yes, we do but we also have trams, taxis, private cars and mini-buses. And, if you have the money to pay, we have helicopters and private aeroplanes.
Visitor   That's interesting and very impressive.
Resident   But, that's not all. There is a very useful and picturesque way to travel to the top of the Peak.
Visitor   By bus?
Resident   Yes, you can, of course, go by bus but I have in mind the famous Peak Tramway. It has been operating since 1888 and, as far as I know, there has never been an accident. These days, you have to queue for quite a long time in order to get a ticket.
Visitor   I expect people will have to queue for the Olympic events as well.
Resident   Yes, they probably will.
Visitor   I believe that the equestrian competitions are to be held in Hong Kong in August. I will certainly try to come.
Resident   You're right. We feel quite privileged to have these competitions. There's no doubt that thousands of visitors who will come here for the Games and also for the shopping. Hong Kong has been described as a shopper's paradise. Our Tourist Board is working very hard to inform people about the Games, about shopping opportunities and, of course about our delightful country parks. We also have two splendid Theme Parks. Disney World on Lantau Island is relatively new. Ocean Park on Hong Kong Island is well established and hugely popular under dynamic management.

Language & other Notes for Olympic Visitors & Hosts

Visitor   I look forward to it all. Now I can't wait until August!

The Cross-country Competition

Visitor	I'm sorry to bother you again, Mr van Grunsven. But could you help me again?
Van Grunsven	Yes, certainly. I'll do my best.
Visitor	As you know, I'm hoping to attend the Olympic dressage and jumping competitions
Van Grunsven	Yes. That's very good. I'm sure you'll enjoy them.
Visitor	I've read somewhere that the dressage competition is also called the *manège*.
Van Grunsven	That's a very old term. We don't use it any more.
Visitor	Oh, I see. Thank you. I'll remember that. Now, just one other question, Mr van Grunsven, if you don't mind. In addition to the dressage and jumping events, I want to go to the cross-country competitions.
Van Grunsven	But they won't be held in Shatin, you know. You'll need to go to a place called Sheung Shui. You can get there by train.
Visitor	Sheung Shui?
Van Grunsven	Yes. It's quite near the border with the Mainland. The cross-country events will take place at the Hong Kong Golf Club and the nearby Jockey Club Beas River Country Club. Both Clubs are in Sheung Shui
Visitor	Thank you very much. You really have been most helpful.
Van Grunsven	Not at all. It's always a pleasure to help anyone who's interested in the Olympic Games.

Language & other Notes for Olympic Visitors & Hosts

What Shatin Can Offer

Visitor   Perhaps you can help me. I'm going to go to Shatin in August to watch the Olympic equestrian events. Is there anything else that I could do in Shatin?

Tourist Guide   Yes, there is. You could visit the Ten Thousand Buddhas Monastery.

Visitor   That would be interesting, I'm sure. How would I get there?

Guide   I think you'd better ask someone in Shatin when you arrive there.

Visitor   Is there anything else that I could do? Are there other places to visit?

Guide   Yes, certainly. If you're interested in shopping, go to Shatin. It has an excellent Mall. Or, if you like museums, you couldn't do better than visit the Hong Kong Heritage Museum. It's a relatively new museum with excellent facilities. I suggest you spend a complete day there. There's a reasonable snack bar on the ground floor and a nice gift shop. I suggest you could set another day aside to visit the Chinese University Art Gallery. It's right next to the Library Building on the University campus. I think that you would find the Gallery to be very interesting.

Visitor   Thank you. Now after I've been to the Chinese University Gallery, how do I get back to Hong Kong?

Guide   You're staying on the "Hong Kong side?"

Visitor   Yes, that's right.

Guide   Well, you should take the train to Kowloon Tong Station; then change trains at Mongkok Station before taking the third train back to Central.

Visitor   Thank you.

Guide   It's a pleasure.

Language & other Notes for Olympic Visitors & Hosts

Marketing the Games

Visitor	I can tell that Hong Kong is a very lively place.
Hong Kong Businesswoman	Yes, you're right. Is this your first visit?
Visitor	Yes, it is and I'm very excited. I've come here to explore the city and I'll be coming here again for the Olympic equestrian competitions. Are you in business here?
Businesswoman	Yes, I am. I'm participating in the equestrian marketing programme, the EMP.
Visitor	The EMP. What's that?
Businesswoman	Its purpose it to give financial, service and technical support to the Olympic Equestrian Events with a particular focus on sponsorship opportunities.
Visitor	What are they?
Businesswoman	Opportunities for companies to contribute financially to the management of the Games.
Visitor	Do they get anything in return?
Businesswoman	Yes, in quite a number of ways. For example, they can use marks of the Beijing Organising Committee to promote and advertise their products.
Visitor	That's very good.
Businesswoman	Yes, it is. I'm sure that the scheme will be of benefit both to the organizers of the Olympics and the individual businesses. According to Mr Timothy Fok, Vice-President of the Equestrian Committee, "Olympic sponsorship is a win-win proposition."

Language & other Notes for Olympic Visitors & Hosts

Getting Around

Visitor	Hong Kong's public transport system seems to be good.
Hong Kong Resident	Yes, it is. It's *very* good. The MTR in particular has been expanding lot recently.
Visitor	The MTR?
Resident	Yes, the Mass Transit Railway. It's has served the people of Hong Kong and many visitors since 1979. It carries over three million passengers every day.
Visitor	Over three million! That's nearly half the population of Hong Kong.
Resident	That's right.
Visitor	Why is the system so popular?
Resident	Well, it's very efficient. The trains run frequently and tickets are not too expensive.
Visitor	Do people still use tickets? In London, we use Oyster cards.
Resident	We don't have Oysters but we do have Octopuses!
Visitor	Octopuses are smart cards?
Resident	Yes, that's right. They're very convenient. I use mine nearly every day, not only on trains but also on buses and in many shops.
Visitor	I must buy one of these cards. Where can I do that?
Resident	At any MTR Station, from the Customer Service counter.
Visitor	Thank you. That's very helpful.

It's the effort that counts

Visitor	I'm going to the Olympics in Hong Kong.
Hong Kong Resident	But most of the events will be held in Beijing.
Visitor	I know but I'm very fond of horses and I only want to see the equestrian competitions.

Language & other Notes for Olympic Visitors & Hosts

Resident	Horses and men.
Visitor	Horses, men and women!
Resident	Of course. And there'll be stallions and mares!
Visitor	Stallions, mares, women and men.
Resident	And geldings, too, I imagine. Yes, all working together with the same objectives, to win Olympic medals, preferably made of gold.
Visitor	Bronze and silver would be all right, too. It's really the effort that counts.
Resident	Yes, you're right.

The Cable Car

Visitor	It's my last day in Hong Kong and I've been on the Peak Tram to say goodbye. It was a beautiful day and the skies were clear.
Hong Kong Resident	I'm glad. Sometimes pollution is a problem and it ruins the view from the top. A ride on the Tram is very enjoyable but when you next come to Hong Kong you'll able to take the cable car, as well.
Visitor	Is this cable car on Hong Kong Island?
Resident	No, it's on Lantau Island.
Visitor	How do I get there?
Resident	There are several ways. I like to take the ferry from Hong Kong Pier Number Three to Discovery Bay. Then I take a bus to the new town of Tung Chung. The cable car building is very near to the bus station.
Visitor	That seems easy enough. Is the cable car ride interesting?
Resident	It certainly is. It's a wonderful journey of about twenty-five minutes over valleys and trees and waterfalls.
Visitor	Is there anything to see at the end of the journey?
Resident	Yes. You'll be able to visit the Po Lin Monastery

Language & other Notes for Olympic Visitors & Hosts

	and also see the Tian Tan Buddha.
Visitor	I've seen other statues of Buddha.
Resident	But this is the largest seated bronze Buddha in the world. It's magnificent.
Visitor	Then I must go before the Olympics.
Resident	Yes. Try to come here before the equestrian events take place. There's a lot to see and experience in Hong Kong. We're proud of our "World City" and visitors are always welcome.

Poster at the former Star Ferry underpass leading to Hong Kong's Central District, which it portrays, December 2007. *Photograph PVHK.*

Language & other Notes for Olympic Visitors & Hosts

Language Five

Important Signs and Notices in English
When you know the meaning of the following words and phrases, you may wish to add them below in your own language.

Be careful! ....
Danger! ....
Do Not Enter! ....

Elevator ....
Emergency Exit ....
Escalator ....
Exit ....
Gentlemen. Gents. ....
Hold the Rail! ....
Hospital. Clinic. ....
Information ....
Keep Off the Grass! ....
Ladies ....
Lavatory/ Lavatories ....
Please let passengers get out first! ....
Lift (Elevator) ....
Men ....
Women ....

Mind the Gap! ....

Money changer. ....

No Entrance ....
No Parking ....
No Spitting ....
No walking on the track! ....
Not For Sale ....

Police Report Station ....
Pull ....
Push ....
Platform. ....
Private ....
Public Convenience(s)
Ticket Counter ....
Toilet(s) ....
Waiting Room ....

Language & other Notes for Olympic Visitors & Hosts

Language Six

Abbreviations for Terms Used at the Olympics

A.A.A.	Amateur Athletic Association
A.A.U	Amateur Athletic Union
AC	Also completed
c	Approximately
C	Number of competitors entered
D	Date of final
Dec.	Won by judges decision
DISC	Discus throw
DISQ	Disqualified
DNC	Did not compete in the final
DNF	Did not finish
DNS	Did not start in final
e	Estimated
elim	Eliminated
EOR	Equalled Olympic record
EWR	Equalled world record
FT	Feet
GA	Goals against
GF	Goals for
GRW	Greco-Roman wrestling
H	Hurdles
HAM	Hammer Throw
HJ	High jump
IN	Inches
JAV	Javelin throw
kg (*sic*)	Kilograms
km	Kilometres
KO	Knockout
L	Lost

Language & other Notes for Olympic Visitors & Hosts

LBS	Pounds
LJ	Long Jump
M (*sic*)	Metres (Meters)
m.p.s.	Metres per second
N	Number of countries represented.
OR	Olympic record
PA	Points against
Pen	Penalty
PF	Points for
PTS	Points
PV	Pole vault
RA	Run against
Ret	Retires
RF	Runs for
RSC	Referee stopped contest
SP	Shot put
T	Number of teams entered
T	Ties
TG	Touches given
TR	Touches received
W	Won
W	Wind-aided
with	Withdrawn
WB	World best
WO	Walkover
WR	World record
YDS	Yards

Language & other Notes for Olympic Visitors & Hosts

Language Seven

Special Words and Expressions Used at the Olympics

Aquatic centre
Call room
Category
Charter eligibility code
Closing ceremony
Coach
Competition
Diplomas
Doping control
Entry standards
Equestrian park
Equipment
Event
Final
First heat
First round
Gender verification test
General cases
Group
Gymnasium
Judges
Medals
Medical controls
National team leader

National uniform
Olympic flag
Olympic song
Olympic souvenirs
Olympic sports
Opening ceremony
Phase
Prizes
Protests
Qualifying round
Qualifying distance
Regulations
Rules
Semi-Final
Souvenirs
Swimming pool
Technical questions
Time-Limit
Timetable
Training facilities
Velodrome
Venues
Warm-up area

Language & other Notes for Olympic Visitors & Hosts

Language Eight

Abbreviations for International Sporting Associations, Committees, Federations, Societies and Unions

AIBA	Amateur International Boxing Association
FIC	International Canoeing Federation
FIAC	International Amateur Cycling Federation
FEI	International Equestrian Federation
FIE	International Fencing Federation
FIFA	International Federation of the Football Association
FIG	International Gymnastics Federation
FIH	International Hockey Federation
FILA	International Amateur Wrestling Federation
FINA	International Amateur Swimming Federation
FISA	International Federation of Rowing Societies
FIVB	International Volley-Ball Federation
IAAF	International Amateur Athletic Federation
IBA	International Baseball Federation
IBF	International Badminton Federation
IJF	International Judo Federation
IOC	International Olympic Committee
ITF	International Tennis Federation
IWF	International Weightlifting Federation
IYRU	International Yacht Racing Union
UIPMB	International Modern Pentathlon and Biathlon Union
UIT	International Shooting Union
WTF	World Taekwondo Federation

Language & other Notes for Olympic Visitors & Hosts

Visitors' Notes 1

Useful Web Sites

Official Web Sites
Beijing 2008 Olympic Games: http://en.beijing2008.cn
Chinese Olympic Committee: http://en.olympic.cn/games
Olympic Movement:
www.olympic.org
www.olympic.org/uk/games/Beijing
www.olympic.org/uk/athletes/results/search_r_uk.asp

Olympic studies website
Hong Kong Baptist University Centre for Olympic Studies:
http://www.hkbu.edu.hk/~hkcos/

Additional Web Sites
Accommodation:
www.accommodation-Olympic-Games.com
www.yurong-europe.com/en/beijing_2008_olympics
Beijing culture: www.thebeijinger.com
Chinese language study and culture: www.linese.com
Complete hotel and airline ticket system: www.chinatravel.com
Comprehensive frequency channel (45 languages):
http://www.cri.cn/index_1.htm
Difficult questions answered: http://www.at0086.com
Direct broadcasting news platform: http://www.chinadaily.com.cn
Economics and culture: www.china.org.cn/english/index.htm
The equestrian events Hong Kong 2008:
http://www.equestrian2008.org/eng/front_e_aspx
The Financial Times: www.ft.com
Information about life in China: www.foreignercn.com
Security: www.security-int.com/news/2007/08/06/beijing-olympic-games
Sports and recreation: www.squidoo.com/china2008
Travel Agent: www.travelchinaguide.com/beijing-olympic

Language & other Notes for Olympic Visitors & Hosts

Visitors' Notes 2

Time Differences and Measurements

Time Differences

Some time differences in Southeast and East Asia, adjusted to Greenwich Mean Time (GMT): –

China + 8 hours   Republic of Korea + hours
India + 5.5 hours   Sri Lanka + hours
Japan + 9 hours   Thailand + 7 hours
Philippines + 8 hours

Some countries adopt Summer (Daylight Saving) Time, i.e. + 1 hour, for part of the year.

Measurements

To convert centimetres into inches, multiply by 039.
To convert inches into centimeters, multiply by 2.54.

1 metre (meter) = 39.37inches / 3.28 feet / 1.09 yards

1 foot= 0.30 metres   1 yard = 0.90 metres

1 kilogram = 2.2 pounds   1 pound = 0.45 kilograms

CAVEAT
Please check all crucial information from other sources. The publishers take no responsibility for any errors or omissions, particularly since circumstances are changing so rapidly.

Forward to Beijing! A Guide to the Summer Olympics

Language & other Notes for Olympic Visitors & Hosts

Visitors' Notes 3

The Olympic Sports

Aquatics: *Swimming*; *Diving*; *Synchronised swimming*;
  Synchronised Diving; Water polo
Archery
Athletics
Badminton
Baseball
Basketball
Boxing
Canoe/Kayak: Flatwater; *Slalom*
Cycling: Track; Road; Mountain Bike; BMX
Equestrian: *Jumping*; *Dressage*; *Eventing*
Fencing
Football (Soccer)
Gymnastics: *Artistic*; *Rhythmic; Trampoline*
Handball
Hockey (Field Hockey)
Judo
Modern Pentathlon
Rowing
Sailing
Shooting: *Rifle*; *Pistol*; *Shotgun*
Softball
Table Tennis
Taekwondo
Tennis
Triathlon
Volleyball: *Indoor*; *Beach*
Weightlifting
Wrestling: *Freestyle*; *Greco-roman*

A Note on Olympic Studies Facilities

An Olympic Studies International Directory (c. 2006)[19] lists 470 authors working on Olympic topics and 379 institutions, either focusing on the Olympics or including Olympic studies, records, or archives, within a broader collection.

The directory identifies nineteen of these as Olympic Studies Centres, which include the IOC Olympic Studies Centre, Switzerland, and Centres in Argentina, Australia, Canada, the Czech Republic, France, Germany, Great Britain, Italy, Korea, New Zealand, The People's Republic of China, Spain, and the Ukraine.

Thirty-three institutions are grouped as holding "Archives and Olympic Heritage" materials, forty-six are identified as Libraries and Information Centres with Olympic materials and thirty-one are named as Research and University Institutions relevant to a study of the Olympic Games.

Among these are the International Olympic Academy and the many national Olympic committees. Institutions such as the Hong Kong Sports Information Centre of the Hong Kong Sports Development Board (set up in 1990) include an Olympic collection within their broader holdings, as does, on a much larger scale, the National Archives of Australia and the Special Collections at the University of California at Los Angeles (UCLA) Library, which includes substantial holdings on the Los Angeles Olympic Games held in each of 1932 and 1984. The holdings of the Olympic Studies Centre of the International Olympic Committee include 900 linear metres of written documents, including the Pierre de Courbertin bequest. There are Olympic Museums too, one of them in Norway.

As long ago as 1988, those eager to support China's participation in the Olympic movement had shown their sincerity by giving financial support to these initiatives. Hong Kong tycoon, Mr Henry Fok, "in the name of the Chinese National

A Note on Olympic Studies Facilities

Olympic Committee", donated HK$8 million towards the construction of the Olympic Museum, then scheduled for completion in 1989 in Lausanne, Switzerland, where the headquarters of the International Olympic Committee is located.[20]

The Directory also lists sixteen relevant "Networks", including for example, The International Society of Olympic Historians, which publishes the ISOH journal and the Sports Philatelists International and the North American Society for Sport History.

Not only, then, do the Olympic Games directly lead to the construction of physical infra-structures such as sports facilities, hotels, improved road and railway networks as well as virtual (telecommunications) networks, they also stimulate the creation of academic facilities such as archives and study centres. For example, Beijing's interest in hosting the Summer Olympics has led to the establishment in the People's Republic of China of the Centre for Olympic Studies, Beijing Sport University (1993) and the Humanistic Olympics Studies Center at the Renmin University (2001). – The website of the Renmin University of China Humanistic Olympics Studies Centre includes news of Olympic related events and reviews of books on Olympic themes. – And at least one more Olympic Studies Centre has come into existence, since this Directory was prepared, in advance of the Beijing Summer Olympics. This is at Hong Kong Baptist University in the Hong Kong Special Administrative Region of the PRC.

KEY TO QUIZZES

CHAPTER ONE
1. 776 BC.
2. Supreme god, god of weather, etc.
3. Sprinting.
4. Poetry.
5. 393 AD.
6. Theodosios I.
7. Panagiotis Soutsos.
8. Much Wenlock, Shropshire, England.
9. 1896.

CHAPTER TWO
1. Lausanne, Switzerland.
2. He stopped rowing to give room for a family of ducks (in 1928).
3. Faster, Higher, Stronger.
4. Eric Liddell; Harold Abrahams.
5. He was helped over the tape.
6. Matthew Arnold.
7. The First World War was in progress.
8. Tarzan.
9. He had accepted travel expenses.
10. Jesse Owens.
11. Mexico was (and still is) a very poor country.
12. The New Zealand team had played Rugby in South Africa, when a boycott was in force because of the Apartheid policy of the South African Government of the time.
13. Because of the Russian invasion of Afghanistan.
14. China.
15. Ben Johnson.

Key to Quizzes

CHAPTER THREE
1. Crown Prince Constantine of Greece (later, King Constantine).
2. She swam the British Channel two hours faster than any man up to that time (1926).
3. For economic reasons.
4. Golf.
5. 1964.

CHAPTER FOUR: Aquatics to Athletics
1. Fifty metres.
2. The "Water Cube".
3. The drugs they took on the advice of the Government appointed sports director and medical director have caused them serious health problems.
4. Four: freestyle, butterfly, back stroke, breast stroke.
5. Seven.
6. Seven.
7. 1900.
8. Four men won two gold medals each.
9. Three.
10. Ten.
11. Seven.
12. (a) archery, (b) athletics, (c) diving, (d) water polo, (e) synchronized swimming

CHAPTER FIVE: Badminton to Cycling
1. "Battledore": in full, "Battledore and shuttlecock".
2. 1972.
3. 1900.
4. Diamonds.
5. The "Mound".
6. Dr James Naismith.
7. Three seconds.

Key to Quizzes

    8. 1996.
    9. Two.
   10. Fighters must wear protective headgear and a vest.
   11. "Repêchage".
   12. An earlier form of bicycle, with one large and one small wheel.
   13. They ride alternately ride slowly and quickly.
   14. Madison Square Garden, New York.
   15. New York.
   16. (a) canoeing/kayak flat water, (b) cycling, (c) badminton, (d) baseball, (e) boxing, (f) beach volleyball, (g) canoeing/kayak (slalom), (h) basketball.

CHAPTER SIX: Equestrian to Football (soccer)
    1. Paris, France (1900).
    2. Three.
    3. Two.
    4. Trot and canter in four different ways.
    5. Three types of sword are used.
    6. Paris (1924).
    7. 1900.
    8. 1996.
    9. Ninety minutes.
   10. Tsu chu.
   11. The first goal scored during extra time.
   12. Sixteen.
   13. Two.
   14. Centre-forward.
   15. (a) football (soccer), (b) equestrian, (c) fencing.

CHAPTER SEVEN: Gymnastics to Judo
    1. 1900.
    2. 2000.
    3. The start value.

Key to Quizzes

    4. Ribbons, hoops, balls. (Two only needed for a correct answer.)
    5. 1976.
    6. Eleven.
    7. Layers of rushes.
    8. According to their weights.
    9. An "ippon" (a match-winning throw or hold scoring ten points).
    10. Four minutes.
    11. (a) rhythmic gymnastics, (b) trampoline, (c) handball, (d) field hockey, (e) judo, (f) artistic gymnastics.

CHAPTER EIGHT: Modern Pentathlon to Softball
    1. Five.
    2. 1,000 points.
    3. 1896.
    4. A light boat used for racing.
    5. 2000.
    6. When the first boat crosses the line.
    7. A shooting competition when the competitor must hold the rifle at his hip until the target is released into the air.
    8. Clay.
    9. The pitcher's "mound" in softball is level with the ground and at a shorter distance from the "home plate" than it is for baseball. Other differences are: the equipment used by the players, the weight and circumference of the ball and the length of play.
    10. (a) rowing, (b) shooting, (c) softball, (d) sailing, (e) pentathlon, (f) equestrian

CHAPTER NINE: Table Tennis to Wrestling
    1. 2004.
    2. 1988.

Key to Quizzes

3. Eleven.
4. 1988.
5. Seven.
6. To kick.
7. The face and the back.
8. Swimming, cycling and running.
9. W. G. Morgan.
10. Spin serve, jump service, "floater".
11. Eight.
12. The wrestler may not hold his opponent in any part of the body below the hips, may not use his legs to press, squeeze or push.
13. (a) table tennis, (b) tennis, (c) weightlifting, (d) wrestling, (e) volleyball, (f) triathlon, (g) taekwondo.

CHAPTER TEN

1. Two hundred and one.
2. 1992.
3. Two.
4. A "green" Olympics.
5. "The Bird's Nest" (National Stadium).
6. Twenty-eight.
7. Three thousand.
8. Shanghai. (He won the gold medal in the 110m final in Athens.)
9. Twenty gold medals. They actually won thirty-two.

References

Beijing Organising Committee for the Games of the XXIX Olympiad. The Official Web Site of the Beijing 2008 Olympic Games.
<http://en.beijing2008.cn/>
Centre d'Estudis Olímpics at the Universitat Autònoma de Barcelona and the Olympic Studies Centre – Olympic Museum Lausanne, *Olympic Studies International Directory* (c. 2006),
<http://www.olympicstudies.uab.es/directory/main.asp>
Finney, Ben. *The Hokule'a: The Way To Tahiti*. New York. Dodd Mead, 1979.
Girardi, W. *Olympic Games*. London: Collins and Franklin Watts, 1972.
Haddon, Celia. *The First Ever Olympic Games*. Hodder and Stoughton, 2004.
[Anon.] "Historic Background", 2003, Chinese Olympic Committee Official Website, 27 March 2004.
Hong Kong Olympic Committee <http://www.hkolympic.org>
[International Olympic Committee,] "Olympic Games Torch-Relay", 9pp.
<http://www.olympic-museum.de/torches/torch1964.htm>
From *Official report 1964*, Vol. 1, pp. 245-268.
Hong Kong Public Records Office (HKPRO), HKRS 545, D & S Nos 1-482, 1964-1986. Nos 3-384, 4-354, 6-361, 7-366, 9-689.
HKPRO, HKRS 70, D & S Nos 1-177. Nos 3-346, 7-92.
Llewellyn Smith, Michael. *Olympics in Athens 1896*. Profile Books Limited, 2004.
South China Morning Post.
South China Morning Post, Calendar for 2008.
Sports Federation & Olympic Committee of Hong Kong, China. Wai Kee Shun and Pang Chung, *Festival of Sport: Golden Jubilee Souvenir Programme*. Hong Kong, 2007.
The Olympic Games: Athens 1896-Athens 2004. Dorling Kindersley Ltd. 2004.
Wellechinsky, David. *The Complete Book of the Summer Olympics*. Sport Classic Books, 2004.
Wenlock Olympian Society website.
<http://www.wenlock-olympian-society.org.uk>
Wikipedia, the free encyclopedia. <http://www.wikipedia.org>
Young, David C. (2004). *A Brief History of the Olympic Games*. Blackwell Publishing, 2004.
Young, David C. *The Modern Olympics: A Struggle for Revival*. The John Hopkins University Press, 1996.

Notes

[1] *The Times*, 27 August 1994
[2] "Hall of Fame" Monash Sport http://www.sport.monash.edu.au/sportsprograms/hall-of-fame.html#7
[3] W. Girardi, *Olympic Games*. London: Collins and Franklin Watts, 1972.
[4] Quoted in Celia Haddon, *The First Ever English Olimpick Games*, Hodder and Stoughton, 2004.
[5] See Celia Haddon, *op. cit.*
[6] Joseph Strutt, *The Sports and Pastimes of the People of England.* London: Printed by T. Bensley for J. White, 1801.
[7] "Olympic Oath", Wikipedia. The reference to doping and drugs first appeared in 2000. Some reference sources have yet to update this information.
[8] "Fundamental Principles of Olympism", *Olympic Charter in force as from 7 July 2007*, International Olympic Committee, October 2007, p. 11, para. 1.
[9] David C. Young, *A Brief History of the Olympic Games*. Blackwell Publishing, 2004, p.151.
[10] Points in this sentence supplied by Helen Clare Cromarty, Wenlock Olympian Society.
[11] *The Wellington Journal and Shrewsbury News*, Saturday October 25th 1890, as recorded in the Wenlock Olympian Society Minute Book 2, p.16. See <http://www.wenlockolympiansociety.org.uk/index.php?pr=The_Archive>
[12] *South China Morning Post*, 14 September 1988.
[13] *South China Morning Post*, 5 September 1964.
[14] Hong Kong Public Records Office, HKRS 545, D & S No. 6-361.
[15] *South China Morning Post*, 5 September 1964.
[16] Li Xiao "China and the Olympic Movement", 5 January 2004, <http://www.china.org.cn/english/olympic/211765.htm#>
[17] *South China Morning Post*, 22 September 1993. Timothy Fok is now also Vice-President of the Olympic Council of Asia (OCA); a Member of the 2008 Olympics Coordination Commission; and Vice President of the Organizing Committee of the 2008 Olympics.
[18] "Proud parents name thousands of children for the Olympics", *South China Morning Post*, 5 November 2007.
[19] Centre d'Estudis Olímpics at the Universitat Autònoma de Barcelona and the Olympic Studies Centre - Olympic Museum Lausanne, Olympic Studies International Directory (c. 2006). <http://www.olympicstudies.uab.es/directory/main.asp>
[20] "Olympic Games and Commonwealth Games, 1988", Hong Kong Public Records Office, HKRS 545 / D & S No. 3/384.

www.ingramcontent.com/pod-product-compliance
Lightning Source LLC
Chambersburg PA
CBHW032126160426
43197CB00008B/532